T0267571

Macbeth

The Applause Shakespeare Workbook Series

OTHER SHAKESPEARE TITLES FROM APPLAUSE

Once More Unto the Speech Dear Friends
in three volumes: *The Comedies, The Histories, The Tragedies*
Compiled and Edited with Commentary by Neil Freeman

Monologues from Shakespeare's First Folio
in twelve volumes: *The Comedies, The Histories, The Tragedies for Any Gender,*
Older Men, Women, and Younger Men
Compiled with Commentary by Neil Freeman, Edited by Paul Sugarman

The Applause First Folio in Modern Type
Prepared and Annotated by Neil Freeman

The Folio Texts
Prepared and Annotated by Neil Freeman
Each of the 36 plays of the Applause First Folio in Modern Type, individually bound

The Applause Shakespeare Library
Plays of Shakespeare Edited for Performance
John Russell Brown, series editor

Shakescenes: Shakespeare for Two by John Russell Brown

Free Shakespeare by John Russell Brown

Shakespeare's Plays in Performance by John Russell Brown

Shakespeare: A Popular Life by Garry O'Connor

The Actor and the Text by Cicely Berry

Acting Shakespeare by John Gielgud

Soliloquy: The Shakespeare Monologues
Co-edited by Michael Earley and Philippa Keil

Macbeth

The Applause Shakespeare Workbook Series

Commentary by
John Russell Brown, Neil Freeman, and R.A. Foakes

Edited by Paul Sugarman

APPLAUSE
THEATRE & CINEMA BOOKS

Essex, Connecticut

APPLAUSE
THEATRE & CINEMA BOOKS

An imprint of Globe Pequot, the trade division of
The Rowman & Littlefield Publishing Group, Inc.
4501 Forbes Blvd., Ste. 200
Lanham, MD 20706
www.rowman.com

Distributed by NATIONAL BOOK NETWORK

Copyright © 2024 by Applause Theatre & Cinema Books

Material drawn from *Shakescenes: Shakespeare for Two*
Copyright © 1992 Applause Theatre Book Publishers

Material drawn from *Once More Unto the Speech Dear Friends*
Copyright © 2006 Folio Scripts, Vancouver, Canada

Material drawn from *Macbeth: The Applause Shakespeare Library*
Copyright © 1996 Applause Books

Introduction and other additional material © 2024 Paul Sugarman

ISBN: 978-1-4930-5704-7 pbk.
ISBN: 978-1-4930-5705-4 epub

All rights reserved. No part of this book may be reproduced in any form or by any electronic or mechanical means, including information storage and retrieval systems, without written permission from the publisher, except by a reviewer who may quote passages in a review.

Library of Congress Cataloging-in-Publication Data
Names: Brown, John Russell, author. | Freeman, Neil, author. | Sugarman,
  Paul, editor.
Title: Macbeth / commentary by John Russell Brown, Neil
  Freeman, and R. A. Foakes ; edited by Paul Sugarman.
Description: Essex, Connecticut : Applause Press, 2023. | Series: Applause
  shakespeare workbook series
Identifiers: LCCN 2023046013 (print) | LCCN 2023046014 (ebook) | ISBN
  9781493057047 (paperback) | ISBN 9781493057054 (epub)
Subjects: LCSH: Shakespeare, William, 1564–1616. Macbeth. | Shakespeare,
  William, 1564-1616—Dramatic production.
Classification: LCC PR2823 .B78 2023 (print) | LCC PR2823 (ebook) | DDC
  822.3/3—dc23/eng/20231002
LC record available at https://lccn.loc.gov/2023046013
LC ebook record available at https://lccn.loc.gov/2023046014

∞™ The paper used in this publication meets the minimum requirements of American National Standard for Information Sciences—Permanence of Paper for Printed Library Materials, ANSI/NISO Z39.48-1992.

CONTENTS

OVERVIEW: WORKING ON SHAKESPEARE TO BUILD TOWARD PERFORMANCE

Perform the Text: Share the text with a wider audience.

Share the Text: Speak the text to someone else.

Action: Find the Choices in the Text: What choices can be made in terms of the character?

Explore the Text: Consult the First Folio to see how capitalization, punctuation, and line endings can shift emphasis. Connect to the text physically and personally.

Analyze the Text: Look at the text in depth to see how it works. Is it verse or prose?

Understand the Text: You need to understand what is being said and what all the words mean.

Read the Text Aloud: These words were meant to be spoken.

INTRODUCTION

Paul Sugarman

The aim of this Applause Shakespeare Workbook is to provide tools for working on the text of *Macbeth*. Out of the many Applause publications on Shakespeare this book draws material from the works of John Russell Brown (*Shakescenes* and the Applause Shakespeare Library) and Neil Freeman (*Once More Unto the Speech* series and the Folio Texts) to give you and/or your actors or students practical approaches to work on the text.

These plays, while they speak much to our human condition today, are from more than four hundred years ago. To fully appreciate Shakespeare, there is a lot that one needs to know. There are many books published by Applause that can help you understand and work on Shakespeare. First you need to understand the time when he lived, which has similarities to today and many differences. *William Shakespeare: A Popular Life* by Garry O'Connor gives insight into Shakespeare's time. Much like Stephen Greenblatt's *Will in the World*, it paints a picture of Shakespeare's age and makes connections between that time and the text in his plays that give a broader perspective on the images and references in Shakespeare's works.

There is the need for much more in-depth study and work on how to use your voice to speak the text. Applause publishes *The Actor and the Text* by Cicely Berry, which reveals how Shakespeare uses language to express so much in such a wide variety of ways and the need to have a strong and connected voice to be able to do it justice. She includes hands-on approaches to the text to show how Shakespeare uses rhetoric to make his points. Her *Working Shakespeare* video series shows many top UK and US actors putting her techniques into practice.

There is also the practicality of how to understand his work in performance. One of John Russell Brown's central ideas is that you can't fully understand and appreciate Shakespeare without understanding how it works in performance. He wrote many books on Shakespeare and many editions of the works of Shakespeare and other early modern playwrights. Applause has published many of his books including

Shakescenes, which provides material for this book; and *Shakespeare's Plays in Performance*, which looks at performance elements and performance history. *Free Shakespeare* contrasts how the plays were originally performed with the vision of the actor-based ensembles, which has been influential for many American acting companies. John Russell Brown created the Applause Shakespeare Library, which included theatrical commentary to make sure that performance considerations are an essential part of studying the play. There is also much that can be gained from great performers of Shakespeare as shown by John Gielgud's books *Acting Shakespeare* and *An Actor and His Time*, as well as the many fine biographies of great stage actors such as Gielgud, Laurence Olivier, and Ralph Richardson, also published by Applause.

The importance of the first collected publication of Shakespeare's plays, the First Folio of 1623, cannot be underestimated. It collected thirty-six of Shakespeare's plays, eighteen of which had never been published before and would have been lost forever. Applause published all thirty-six plays from the First Folio in individual editions that were prepared and annotated by Neil Freeman. Applause published the single volume *The Applause First Folio of Shakespeare in Modern Type*. Freeman then went on to create the *Once More Unto the Speech* series of books comparing modern and Folio texts for more than nine hundred speeches, demonstrating the practicality of using Folio texts. Material from that series has been made more accessible in the recent series of *Monologues from Shakespeare's First Folio* series of twelve books. Neil Freeman was one of the major forces in making the First Folio more useful for actors and students of the plays.

Both John Russell Brown and Neil Freeman were champions for understanding Shakespeare through performance. John Russell Brown's Applause Shakespeare Library was designed to make one aware of the many opportunities presented by the text for performance. Neil Freeman's First Folio texts showed the many clues and choices that could be explored through looking at the text as originally printed. By taking examples from both men's work, these materials present different perspectives on the text.

The wonderful thing about working on Shakespeare is that there is no one "right" answer. His work endures because it is so flexible and subject to varied interpretations. In your own exploration of the text you have to find which choices work best for you (and, perhaps, your students). To find the best choice you need to explore what is out there and why these more than four-hundred-year-old texts still speak to us today.

This workbook presents a brief description of various approaches to the text by John Russell Brown and Neil Freeman. Following are scenes from the play that John Russell Brown had included in *Shake-scenes* along with further selections from the Applause Shakespeare Library edition of the play. Speeches from the play drawn from Neil Freeman's *Once More Unto the Speech* series will give a First Folio perspective on the text.

The goal is to be able to speak and share Shakespeare's words in a way that makes the plays come alive in ways they do not when read silently. Perhaps the biggest perceived challenge is understanding and getting comfortable with Shakespeare's language. Though the language may seem old to us, the English language of Shakespeare was four hundred years *younger* then than it is now, as Kristin Linklater, author of *Freeing Shakespeare's Voice*, observed. Although these words are from four centuries ago, it is still Modern English but in its infancy, when it was still blossoming and expanding. The spoken word was essential to almost all communication in Shakespeare's day, unlike our predominantly visual and text-based age. We don't talk as much or as precisely as those whose lives depended on spoken communication in Shakespeare's time. Shakespeare does a lot more with language than we do in our modern world. Working on Shakespeare's language can open one up to new and more effective ways of communicating. These great thoughts and words show the possibilities of expression that a human voice can achieve.

Basic Steps to Working on Shakespeare's Text

Read the Text Aloud: These words were meant to be spoken. Music cannot be experienced solely by looking at annotations on a page. Neither can Shakespeare.

Understand the Text: You need to understand what is being said and what all the words mean. It is important to consult glossaries that give Elizabethan definitions and context. David and Ben Crystal's website shakespeareswords.com is a good place to start.

Analyze the Text: Look at the text in depth to see how it works. Is it verse or prose? If verse, where is it regular and where not? Shakespeare uses rhetorical devices to convey feelings and meanings. How do the sounds and words "play" off each other?

Explore the Text: Consult the First Folio to see how capitalization, punctuation, and line endings can shift emphasis. Connect to the text physically and personally. How do the words and sounds feel inside your body?

Action: Find the Choices in the Text: What choices can be made in terms of the character? What actions can they take? What choices can be made about their needs? Some choices may seem obvious, but look for the possibilities of different ones.

Share the Text: Speak the text to someone else so that you can assess how well you are communicating the thoughts beneath the text.

Perform the Text: Share the text with a wider audience, to whom you can also speak directly, as there was no fourth wall in Shakespeare's theater.

Committing to speaking Shakespeare's text requires more of us than most contemporary communication does. Energize the whole body when giving voice to the text. There have been many fine books on using the voice to support Shakespeare text work including *The Actor and the Text* by Cicely Berry (Applause) and *Freeing Shakespeare's Voice* by Kristin Linklater (TCG).

The exploration of the text can continue indefinitely as there is no one answer to these texts but an endless array of possibilities to be explored. However, if you start with speaking and listening instead of just reading the words, it will lead you to a more personal connection to the text.

Shakespeare connects to so many people in different ways because we find something in our personal lives that is explained by the way Shakespeare says it. Sometimes the text instantly makes sense to you, but often the possibilities are infinite. We make choices based on how the text connects to us at this moment in our time.

This workbook will outline some of the tools to look at the text and give examples from the works of John Russell Brown and Neil Freeman, who can offer differing viewpoints on the same text as a way for you to learn to trust your ear and your connection to the text. This workbook will show ways to work on the text with a spirit of exploration.

ORIGINAL PRACTICES AND CUE SCRIPTS

Paul Sugarman

What do we know of the original practices of Shakespeare's time? Most of the evidence we have comes from Philip Henslowe, who was the owner of the Rose Theatre. His "diary," which was a log book of receipts for shows that they would perform 6 days a week, including many different plays. In a month where they could do 24–27 performances they would stage 15–20 different plays with only a few repeated more than once. We have little documentation on the rehearsal and performance practices of the time, but we are able to get an idea of how they worked from references in plays (such as the Mechanicals rehearsals in *A Midsummer Night's Dream*) and the papers left by Edward Alleyn, Henslowe's son-in-law and the lead actor of The Lord Admiral's Men.

Edward Alleyn was, along with Richard Burbage, one of the leading actors of Shakespeare's time. Alleyn founded Dulwich College, to which he bequeathed papers from his theatrical career, including Henslowe's diary, a cue script from *Orlando Furioso* and a platt (scene plot) for *The Seven Deadlie Sinnes* from which scholars have deduced what we know of the rehearsal practices of the day. Instead of receiving the full text, the actors would get a cue script which had their lines and the line that came before their line (their cue). A platt was a listing of all the scenes with entrances and sound cues that would be hung backstage for the cast to refer to.

The cue scripts were hand-written by copyists. By just giving the actors their lines and cues it was easier for the company than providing a whole script. Also, it allowed the company to maintain tighter control over the complete text of a play since copyright didn't really exist back then. If a rival company of actors got hold of a play text there would be nothing to stop them from performing it. Full scripts were kept under lock and key at the theatre.

Cue scripts have enjoyed something of a renaissance with Patrick Tucker (another contemporary champion of the First Folio). The Original Shakespeare Company created by Tucker did performances using scrolls with very minimal rehearsal to mimic the conditions under which the plays might usually have been done.

A number of Shakespeare companies work with cue scripts. Cue script Shakespeare performances have been presented by many companies that did readings from scrolls, including the Actors Shakespeare Company and Spontaneous Shakespeare. For readings they are quite useful as they are compact enough that one can move easily with them and it can look more like a performance than a reading in which actors are carrying around conspicuous scripts.

They are very useful for learning lines, as you can focus solely on your cues, dialogue, and speeches. They are convenient to carry around. There are a number of actors who have told me that they set up cue scripts when they're doing contemporary plays as well, as they are just a useful mechanism for learning lines. In Shakespeare's time, scrolls were also referred to as "rolls," and it is possible that the term "roles" came from this usage.

How to Make Your Own Scrolls

One can make up one's own scrolls for parts with an electronic version of the text.

The materials needed are quite readily available except for the dowels which form their basis. I have seen people make scrolls of unsharpened pencils, but those are too short and thin for an effective scroll base. You need two ½-inch dowels 8–9-inches long, paper, scissors, scotch tape, and covered hair elastics. (Dowel rods come in varying lengths; you can get several scrolls from one rod.)

Of course, once you make a digital cue script you can read it on your phone or mobile device. However, I find that having a physical scroll leads to quicker memorization.

Starting with the digital file for the script, using Word or similar software, just cut out everyone else's lines except for their cues for your character's lines. A cue wouldn't be the full prior speech but just the last 3–5 words of their speech.

The text should be formatted so that it is in a large enough font to be easily readable and formatted so that it is no wider than 5-inches wide.

Print out your scroll, trim the paper so that it is about 6–6½ inches wide, and tape it to one of the dowels. As you trim the pages, tape them together so that they flow continuously. While you add to your role you can roll what you have done on to the dowel and secure it with a binder clip to keep it from unrolling. When you get to the end of the end of your role, you tape it to the other dowel.

Then you use the hair rubber bands to hold the dowels together and move back and forth in the part. As you become comfortable you can easily advance the scroll with one hand.

ADVICE TO ACTORS

John Russell Brown

There is no such person as a "Shakespearean actor," if that phrase implies the possession of unique qualifications or unusual gifts. Shakespeare's plays are available to all good actors, no matter what their training or experience may be.

Yet, of course, the texts reprinted here are not like those of modern plays. Shakespeare does present special problems, and the blunt assurance that his writing is open for anyone to explore will not sound very convincing to a student-actor meeting it for the first time. The following approaches are offered as encouragement to make a start and free imagination to work intelligently on the texts.

Character

First of all, an actor in any play must discover the person behind the words of any particular role. Of course, an actor must learn how to speak the character's lines clearly and forcefully, but that alone will not bring the play to life. Speech is not all, because Shakespeare did not write for talking heads. He first imagined individual persons in lively interplay with each other and *then* conjured words for them to speak; and that is the best sequence for an actor to follow. A living person has to be brought to the stage, and then he can begin to speak and become realized in the process.

In Elizabethan times, plays were performed on a large platform stage that jutted out into the middle of a crowded audience, many of whom were standing rather than sitting as is the custom today; and in this open arena everything took place by daylight. Some performances were given indoors, but then the audience was illuminated along with the actors. Such conditions were more like those of a public meeting in our day, or of a booth in a fairground. They called for an acting style that was grounded in a basic physical delineation of each character. An actor had to maintain the vibrant outlines of the role so that his performance could be viewed from all sides and at all times whenever he was on stage.

Character Questions

BASIC QUESTIONS:

- How does the character move and speak?

- How think and feel?

- Where does this individual come from? What does he know? What does he want?

- What does he look like, sound like?

- How could anyone recognize the person who speaks these lines?

- Why does this particular person need to speak these particular words?

- How old is this person?

- What physical characteristics are essential for an impersonation?

- What is this person's family situation?

- What are the political, professional, and social conditions of his life?

MORE DIFFICULT QUESTIONS FOLLOW, WHICH HELP TO DEFINE PERSONALITY AND CONSCIOUSNESS:

- How does this person "see" and respond to the world around him?

- What does he like and dislike? What does he pursue and what does he seek to avoid?

- What conventions, social pressures, or political forces influence behavior, either consciously or unconsciously?

INTERROGATING THE TEXT:

- What verbs does the character use?

- How does he talk to other characters?

- Do questions, assertions, explanations, answers, excuses, qualifications, elaborations, or repetitions predominate?

- Are sentences long or short, leisured and assured, or compact and urgent?

- Are sentences governed by a single main verb?

- Or are they supplied with a sequence of phrases, each governed by its own subsidiary verb?

- How does this person refer to others: always in the same way, or with variations? With different names, titles, or endearments?

- Is address intimate or formal, simple or elaborate?

- Or is contact between two characters assumed and assured, so that names are not required at all?

Normally such detailed verbal enquiry is a continuous process that goes on throughout a long rehearsal period. Scrutiny of every word in even a short scene will help to develop a sensitivity to words, a facility that can be drawn upon constantly throughout an actor's career in whatever plays he may perform.

ALL KINDS OF EXERCISES CAN HELP:

- Very slow rehearsals encourage full awareness of what is thought and felt, as the words are spoken easily without thought of projecting or shaping them.

- Silent rehearsals, with someone else speaking the text.

- Improvised explorations of moments of encounter or retreat.

- Improvised paraphrasing of Shakespeare's text.

- Sessions in which the actors sit back-to-back and only speak the words, trying to communicate fully.

- Variations in positions, so that the two actors are at first close and then far apart, quite still and then always on the move, looking at each other or refusing to do so, paying attention to nothing but the sound of words or engaged on other business—all these explorations may find new means of expression or more physical enactments for a scene.

- Questions should be asked, as for any play, to encourage a fuller sense of what is afoot in a scene: What do they expect from each other? How secure or insecure are they?

What we can deduce about Elizabethan stage practice should encourage present-day actors to seek out distinctive physical characteristics for each role they play in Shakespeare, possess or embody them as fully as possible, and then play the text boldly. This will provide the appropriate dynamic and credibility.

The moment actors walk onto the stage in character, they must be strong and expressive, even before a word has been spoken. Then as each person is drawn into the drama, there must be no loss of definition but growth, development, and surprise. As the play continues, new facets and new resources will be revealed, until each character has become fully present and open to an audience. In performance, actors need to be alert and active and must possess great reserves of energy. They are like boxers in a ring who dare not lose concentration or the ability to perform at full power. They have to watch, listen, move, and speak, and at the same time embody the persons they represent. It is like levitating, or flying through the air, by a continuous act of will and imagination. Characters must have clarity; actors, courage.

But how can an actor find the person to present? Trial and error play no small role in shaping a trained instinct for Shakespeare's people. And this trial begins with a close interrogation of the text.

In a search for the person to bring onstage, first impressions may be deceptive or, rather, limiting. For example, on a first reading, Romeo and Juliet may appear to be two "typical" romantic lovers who delight in each other's presence and have much in common, including parents who would disapprove very strongly of their love if they were to know of it. All that is true and useful, but if the two actors for these roles were each to make a list of the nouns in their respective speeches, two very different sensibilities and personalities would be revealed. The minds of Romeo and Juliet run in different directions; they have their own sensations and feelings, and distinct views of the world around them.

There are many constructive ways of studying Shakespeare's words beyond tracing verb patterns. Preparing lists of adjectives and adverbs may reveal when and where a character is sufficiently thoughtful to qualify an idea, although some speakers in some scenes will never have sufficient command or perception to use a qualifying or descriptive word. Lists of double meanings, similes, metaphors, references to other realities than the one on-stage—whether the imagined world is distant, intimate, literary, political, religious, or historical—can help to show the deeper resources of a character's mind.

Slowly, by such analysis of the text, a psychological "identikit" can be assembled, marking predominant colors, preconceptions, modes of thought and feeling. Many such separate and small details begin to suggest a more embracing idea about a person.

On the other hand, it would be a mistake to read and analyze for too long; an actor needs to start to act and to speak just as soon as intuition and imagination are quickened by more deliberate investigations. The actor's own being has to be satisfied and used in performance, as well as the details of the text.

Slowly, a sense of the character's consciousness will emerge, and a number of physical traits will become established. So, the stage character should evolve slowly, from within itself, freshly and uniquely created; actions will suit the words and reveal a sense of being that attracts and repays attention. There is no knowing what may happen. One danger is that too many details will attract attention so that the basic presence is left undeveloped. After making his discoveries, the actor must therefore decide which of his discoveries are truly necessary and which can be discarded.

Careful and patient study, analysis, exploration, imitation, quiet impulse, quick imagination, and the luck of adventurous rehearsal all have a contribution to make in the creation of these plays.

Verse, Prose, and Language

Laurence Olivier in his portrayal of the lead in *Henry the Fifth* decided to be real, rather than phony, grand, or rhetorical. So he "got underneath the lines," and in rehearsal his acting became so close to natural behavior that the words were sometimes indistinct and difficult to hear. Then one day, Tyrone Guthrie, the director, stopped the rehearsal—he had been away for a while and insisted that this actor should perform the verse and the rhetoric: "Larry . . . let's have it properly," he called out from the back of the theater. For a moment, Olivier hesitated and then did as he was told; and the change, as he tells the story, was instantaneous and transforming. He had always known that verse and sentence structure, and imagery, were instructing him to speak with confidence, enjoyment, and resonance, and that they had a commanding and developing power, but he had held back in distrust. Now he found that artificial verse and grand language fitted his character like necessary and proper clothes, and they gave him the ability to rouse his audience on stage and in the auditorium. (When he came to act the part in the film, they even roused his horse.) Olivier was still truth-ful, but now he was also heroic.

Poetry is the natural idiom of Shakespeare's stage, as swimming is for the ocean, singing for opera or musical theater, controlled and exceptional movement for dance, or solemnity for great occasions. Speaking Shakespeare's verse becomes as instinctive as song, and the actor forgets that he is being metrically correct and vocally subtle.

Elizabethan audiences were so convinced by performances in which verse was spoken that a play written wholly in prose would be more likely to seem artificial. Today Shakespeare's plays can become *just* as real, if actors both use the verse and also act with truth to life. Bernard Shaw advised actors in Shakespeare's early plays to treat the verse like a child does a swing, without self-consciousness or hesitation. In later plays the art of verse is more demanding and the pleasure it gives deeper, but both must be similarly instinctive.

Until verse speaking has become second nature—as it quite quickly does—an actor should study the meter of the lines well in advance of rehearsals, methodically picking out the words to be stressed and find-ing, by trial and error, the most appropriate phrasing. It is necessary to speak the lines out loud, so that meaning and syntax can be related to the demands of versification and *vice versa*. Breathing and speaking should work together so that the energy of thought and feeling responds to the text and begins to motivate speech. Texture, linked variations of sound, alliteration, assonance, rhyme, and rhythm must all be heeded. These concepts cannot be explored fully in the mind. By speaking the words, their sounds and visceral impact will reveal different levels of meaning. Phrasing, breathing, tempo, pace, pitch, intonation, silence have all to be considered. The lines must be spoken aloud again and again, as one way of speaking is tested against another; and then, slowly, by following the clues inherent in the text, a fully responsive delivery can emerge.

When using this book, start to "do" whenever doubt arises. Genera-tions of actors will assure you that with practice, the acting of Shake-speare's poetry—not merely the speaking of it—becomes instinctive and fluent, pleasurable and, in the context of the play, both true and natural.

The actor should begin by appreciating Shakespeare's preferred medium, the iambic pentameter. Each line should have ten syllables, alter-nately weak and strong, so that each pair of syllables forms one "foot," and five feet complete a line. Although few pentameters are entirely regular—

if they were, the dialogue would be unbearably wooden and predictable—all follow the ongoing pattern to some degree. It is their likeness that links them together, while their irregularity draws attention to particular words, varies rhythm and pace, and lends a forward movement to speech as disturbance of pattern awakens an expectation that pattern will be reasserted and finally satisfied.

Steps to analyzing the text

- Is it verse or prose?
- If verse, is it regular or irregular? Many lines are irregular with stresses not following the iambic pattern or if there are other than ten syllables in a line.
- Speak the text to find the most natural emphasis.

Sense, syntax, speakability, and an underlying regularity are the principal guides in scanning a line, but they do not always provide an unequivocal lead. Until well-practiced in verse speaking, a student should mark the text in pencil, changing the stresses until sure enough to start rehearsals. Still more changes may be made later, before this slow and methodical preparation can be forgotten and taken for granted—that is the last and absolutely necessary part of the process.

Scansion

In deciding how to scan a line, some general rules may be applied. Nouns and verbs always need to be stressed in order to make the sense clear—more stressed than adjectives, adverbs, pronouns, prepositions, or conjunctions. Moreover the fourth syllable of any line, being the most able to reestablish the normal pattern after irregularities and most in control of each individual line, is nearly always stressed in a regular way. If the end of a line is irregular, the beginning of the following one is likely to be regular, for two, or three, consecutive feet. However, the first foot in a line is very frequently irregular, since a reversed foot, with the strong syllable coming first, gives fresh impetus to new thought.

An example from an early play gives clear indication of both regularity and irregularity:

(King Edward speaks to his queen about political enemies.)

˘ — ˘ — ˘ — ˘ — ˘ — —
My love, forbear to fawn upon their frowns.

˘ — ˘ — ˘ — ˘ — ˘ — ˘
What danger or what sorrow can befall thee

˘ — ˘ — ˘ — ˘ — ˘ —
So long as Edward is thy constant friend

˘ — ˘ — ˘ — ˘ — ˘ —
And their true sovereign whom they must obey?

— ˘ ˘ — ˘ — ˘ — — —
Nay, whom they shall obey, and love thee too,   5

˘ — ˘ — ˘ — ˘ ˘ — —
Unless they seek for hatred at my hands-

˘ — ˘ — ˘ ˘ — ˘ — —
Which if they do, yet will I keep thee safe

˘ — ˘ — ˘ — ˘ ˘ — —
And they shall feel the vengeance of my wrath.

*(Henry VI, Part 3, IV.i.*75–82)

Some of the strong stresses marked in these lines might be changed, but very few; and all its irregularities are brief. The close of line 5 is most problematical: it is marked here with three consecutive strong syllables as the sense of the parenthesis seems to require, but the final "too" might be unstressed or, possibly, the penultimate "thee." (Three consecutive strong stresses should be used very sparingly, because they doubly disturb the underlying norm.) A similar uncertainty arises at the end of line 2, which is marked here with the final "thee" as an extra unstressed syllable. Alternatively, "can" would not be stressed and "befall" counted as a single strong syllable, so that "thee" could follow with equal stress.

All the strong syllables are not equally stressed in speech, and here actors have much more liberty to find the emphasis that suits their own interpretation of a character. Many choices are available. In most iambic pentameters only three syllables take major emphasis, the other stressed syllables being only slightly more prominent than the unstressed ones. So one reading of the same passage might be:

My love, *forbear* to *fawn* upon their *frowns.*
What *danger* or what sorrow can *befall* thee

So *long* as Edward is thy constant friend
And their true sovereign whom they *must obey?*
Nay, whom they *shall* obey, and *love thee* too,
Unless they *seek* for *hatred* at my *hands*
Which if they *do,* yet will I *keep* thee *safe*
And they shall feel the *vengeance* of my *wrath.*

Perhaps the first line should have four major emphases, as Edward presses his argument. In line 3, "constant" may be more significant than "long" and so take the emphasis; but the "f" in *friend* makes that word able to gain strength from the other stressed *f*s in the preceding lines. Choice of stress will also be influenced by words set either in opposition to contrast with each other or in agreement to reinforce each other. Stressing these words can often clarify the logic of what the speaker is saying. For example, in line 4, "their" might be stressed and the penultimate foot reversed, so that "they" is stressed as well for reinforcement, and "must" would count only as a weak syllable. Such a reading would raise the possibility that in line 7, "thee" might be stressed rather than "keep," so that the "they" in line 8 could be a fourth major emphasis in contrast with "thee," to bring a relatively sturdy finish to the whole speech. But, in general, pronouns should not be emphasized, because that takes away prominence from the nouns and verbs, which have to sustain the sense of any speech; those are the elements that form the supporting backbone for strong dialogue and provide its thought-action and forward impetus.

This simple speech of eight lines illustrates how metrical consider-ations become, very quickly and necessarily, issues of character as well. The same is true when problems of phrasing are introduced. In the early verse plays especially, a brief pause at the end of each line is usual and provides a further guide to phrasing beyond those inherent in sense and syntax. Yet this is not a constant rule, and sometimes only the slight-est rise of pitch or marking of a final consonant is sufficient indication of a line-ending; in this way, two consecutive lines will run into each other almost without hesitation or change of impression. In this pas-sage, if Edward pauses slightly after "friend," the last word of line 3, and after "safe" at the end of line 8, his thoughts of "love" will seem more urgent than those concerning political power because, in this reading, the latter will seem to be afterthoughts. But if line 3 runs over into line 4, without the customary pause at the line-ending, the two reactions become almost inseparable; and then the political motivation will out-weigh the amorous, because it is expressed in a longer phrase and placed in a climactic position. The relationship between lines 7 and 8 raises similar possibilities.

A pause, or caesura, may also be marked in mid-line. Syntax or sense will sometimes require this to be done (as in line 7 above), but here too a choice is often to be made. The advantage of a mid-line break is that it can give a sense of ongoing thought and quick intelligence. Some critics would argue that every line should have its caesura, but there is good reason not to supply them too strongly or too consistently; such readings encourage a halting delivery and an impression of weakness, and are not always easy to comprehend. In this passage, the final line would clearly be stronger if there were no hint of a pause in mid-line. So might line 2—unless two slight pauses were given, as if commas had been placed after both "danger" and "sorrow," thus giving Edward a very thoughtful and determined manner of speech. Line 6 also seems to run without a break, unless it came after "seek," so giving point to Edward's personal involvement. Seldom should a mid-line pause be placed so that it breaks up a regular iambic foot; normally it should follow, and therefore still further emphasize, a strong syllable. If a caesura is marked in each line of this passage, a general impression of energetic thought might be given, and in some performances this could be useful.

No decision is solely a technical matter; versification in Shakespeare's mind was an instrument for enhancing a representation of individual characters in lively interplay. Problems of verse-speaking are truly dramatic problems, and so each actor must find solutions that suit his or her own impersonation. Although there are many ways of speaking verse that are clearly wrong—too many stressed syllables one after another is a common fault, and too few clear stresses another—there is no one correct way to speak any speech. A respect for versification offers many opportunities to strengthen one's grasp of the play in action and deepen the rendering of a character's very being.

As in any lifelike dialogue in prose, the actor must ask why speak at all; that is, he must discover and follow the action of thought and feeling beneath the words, sustaining and shaping them. In other terms, syntax is, in the last analysis, more important than meter. Each complete sentence is a distinct action, requiring breath, physical response, and speech, according to its own impulses.

In prose dialogue, sentence structure is the principal means whereby Shakespeare controls and so strengthens an actor's speaking of his text. Often the formal arrangement is very elaborate and sustained. Moreover, its effect is reinforced by the use of a series of parallel phrases and by wordplay; these both hold the subsections together and provide a sense of growth and climax. Exploring how the words play off each other in these ways can reveal the character's intentions. Stressing key words, puns, and affirmations is not enough; the flow and energy of the language have to be represented in performance, giving a sense of exploration, energy, struggle, attainment, frustration. Sentence structure and wordplay define this music and this drama, and the actor must respond to both and transmit both through performance.

Each actor must make his own distinctive response to the challenge of the text. No teacher or director can provide ready-made and sufficient solutions here, and this realization may help to understand something fundamental about the acting of Shakespeare: no instruction can take responsibility away from the actors. Sometimes students are recommended to speak Shakespeare's lines with a certain quality or tone of voice, or a certain accent, and for some exercises or some productions this may be useful. But following such a prescription is likely to do more harm than good, because the actor is distracted from the primary task of finding a voice and being for each character and then responding to the text in his or her own manner. Of course, efficient breathing and voice production are needed to respond to so demanding a text, but technical expertise must always be at the service of the specific demands of character, situation, and speech, as these are discovered by each individual actor.

Some words and phrases in the plays seem to cry out for a great deal of preparatory work, but it may be only a small exaggeration to say that every word, phrase, sentence, and speech may repay in some measure a similar investment. An actor can have an endless adventure when acting Shakespeare, as step by step he gets closer to a fully responsive, individual, and necessary (and therefore convincing) way of turning text into performance.

An actor's mind and body need to be more than usually alert and energized to answer the challenge. What starts as patient and complicated exploration can end, however, in a marvelous extension of an actor's powers of thought, feeling, and being, as the poetry comes to fresh and brilliant life. That is why Shakespeare's plays are so rewarding to perform. By making each word sound as if it is necessary to his or her character, an actor will claim attention with amazing ease.

Toward Performance

All kinds of exercises can help inexperienced actors. Very slow rehearsals encourage full awareness of what is thought and felt, as the words are spoken easily without thought of projecting or shaping them. Silent rehearsals, with someone else speaking the text, improvised explorations of moments of encounter or retreat, improvised paraphrasing of Shakespeare's text, or sessions in which the actors sit back-to-back and only speak the words, trying to communicate fully—all these devices may help performers to become more free, adventurous, and true. Variations in positions, so that the two actors are at first close and then far apart, quite still and then always on the move, looking at each other or refusing to do so, paying attention to nothing but the sound of words or engaged on other business—all these explorations may find new means of expression or more physical enactments for a scene. Questions should be asked, as for any play, to encourage a fuller sense of what is afoot in a scene: What do they expect from each other? How secure or insecure are they? Many of these questions were first asked in individual preparation. None of these ordinary ways of working is foreign to Shakespeare's plays.

When performing modern plays, actors have extensive stage directions in the text to guide them: descriptions of activity, unspoken reactions, movements, pauses, silences, and so on. But in Shakespeare's plays there is little of this, and what is printed in modern editions is often the invention of editors and not what Shakespeare wrote. In the versions of scenes printed in this book, stage directions are very scarce and minimal, but the commentary will often point out activity, movement and responses, that *may* be required for acting the text.

Actors must learn to read Shakespeare's stage directions implicit in the dialogue: clues for tempo, rhythm change, breathing, for closeness or distance between the characters, and so on. Very important, because usually unambiguous, is Shakespeare's use of incomplete verse lines to indicate a pause or silence in the middle of speech, or in the interchange between two people. When two characters share a single verse line, each speaking one half of a regular iambic pentameter, the opposite is true; there should be no pause or hesitation here, the dialogue continuing without break and the new speaker responsive to the phrasing, rhythm, and pitch of the person he follows.

So much can be discovered while working together on a text that simplification must become part of the ongoing process. Actors must identify those elements that are truest and most revealing and develop those at the cost of losing others. The essential part of this process is to recognize what is particularly alive and new in the work and take the necessary steps to allow this to grow.

There is a paradox at the heart of what can be said about the task of acting Shakespeare's plays. Imaginatively the performers need to be exceptionally free, and yet the most liberating work will be found by paying strict attention to the minutest details of the text and using them as spurs to invention and exploration. Shakespeare's imagination seems always to be ahead of ours, beckoning us; and so, if the actor is patient and adventurous, he will find within the text whatever suits his or her individual abilities and point of view. The text can be ever new, and even the most experienced actor or playgoer is liable to be amazed at what is achieved for the first time with any new production.

Of course, actors develop particular ways of working, and their interpretations of a number of roles will have much in common, but it is wise to beware of drawing the possibilities of a Shakespeare text down to the level of performance that a particular actor has found to be reliable. Shakespeare's kings are all different from each other, and so are his fools; and each one is liable to have a different life from scene to scene, sometimes even moment by moment. Even such clear distinctions as that between comedy and drama should be treated with reserve: in important ways, there are no comic and no serious roles in Shakespeare. Hamlet or Prince Hal, Romeo or Juliet all need to raise laughter and act the fool, drawing on skills that are sometimes considered to be appropriate to comedy. Lady Macbeth and Macbeth are deeply involved in a terrible action, but their minds move with swiftness and fantasy, so they play with words, very like witty persons in a comedy. In all Shakespeare's roles, villain or hero, lover or fool, an actor must be ready to respond outside conventional limitations.

When Shakespeare's Prince Hamlet tried to instruct the players who arrived in the court of Elsinore, he was concerned with their technique and their attention to the text, but "their special observance," he said, should be with "nature":

> for anything so o'erdone is from the purpose of playing,
> whose end, both at the first and now, was and is to hold, as
> 'twere, the mirror up to nature. . . .
>
> *(Hamlet*, III.ii.1 ff.)

The key phrase, "hold the mirror up to nature," sounds like a generalized instruction: show everyone what they look like, but in context it is precise. Hamlet is in the process of castigating actors' faults and he continues in the same vein:

> O there be players that I have seen play—and heard others
> praise, and that highly—not to speak it profanely, that, nei-
> ther having th'accent of Christians, nor the gait of Chris-
> tian, pagan nor man, have so strutted and bellowed that I
> have thought some of Nature's journeymen had made men,
> and not made them well, they imitated humanity so
> abominably.

The actors have to "make men"; they have to be highly skilled craftsper-sons, not ordinary workmen ("journeymen"). Characters have to move and speak, and function, as we do: they have been individually crafted and must be alive with individuality. Slowly, skillfully, and adventurously, an actor must build an illusion of a living being, one for whom Shakespeare's text is a necessary extension of existence. Hamlet does not speak for Shakespeare, but in creating this character the dramatist wrote with such freedom, precision, and obvious pleasure that he must have drawn more deeply than usual on his own ideas and reactions. Lacking Shakespeare's advice to the players, Hamlet's is a good substitute.

Another Perspective

Neil Freeman

For another perspective on this famous speech, here is Neil Freeman's Folio version of the text with his commentary:

SPEAKE THE SPEECH I PRAY YOU, AS I PRONOUNC'D 3.2.1–45

Background: Just before the playing of the requested "The Murther of Gonzago" (with "some dosen or sixteene lines" added by Hamlet for Claudius's benefit), Hamlet seems to feel the need to instruct the actors in their business (or as the scholars suggest, Shakespeare felt the need to remind *his* own actors of *their* craft, which some of them seem to have neglected).

Style: general address to a small group
Where: somewhere near the great hall of the castle
To Whom: the first player and colleagues (an unspecified number)
# of Lines: 40   **Probable Timing:** 2.00 minutes

Hamlet

1   Speake the Speech I pray you, as I pronounc'd
it to you trippingly on the Tongue : But if you mouth it,
as many of your Players do, I had as live the Town-Cryer
had spoke my Lines : Nor do not saw the Ayre too much [ ]
your hand thus, but use all gently ; for in the verie Torrent,
Tempest, and (as I may say) the Whirle-winde of [ ]
Passion, you must acquire and beget a Temperance that
may give it Smoothnesse .

2   O it offends mee to the Soule, to
[see] a robustious Pery-wig-pated Fellow teare a Passion to tatters, to verie ragges, to split the eares of the
Groundlings : who (for the most part) are capeable of
nothing, but inexplicable dumbe shewes, & noise : I [could]
have such a Fellow whipt for o're-doing Termagant : it
out-Herod's Herod .

3   Pray you avoid it .

———————————————————

4 Be not too tame neyther : but let your owne
Discretion be your Tutor .

5   Sute the Action to the Word,
the Word to the Action, with this speciall observance : That
you [ore-stop] not the modestie of Nature ; for any

thing so [over-done], is [frö] the purpose of Playing, whose
end both at the first and now, was and is, to hold as 'twer
the Mirrour up to Nature ;   to shew Vertue her owne
Feature, Scorne her owne Image, and the verie Age and
Bodie of the Time, his forme and pressure .

6   Now, this
over-done, or come tardie off, though it [make] the unskil-
full laugh, cannot but make the Judicious greeve ; The
censure of the which One, must in your allowance o're-
way a whole Theater of Others .

7   Oh, there bee Players that
I have seene Play, and heard others praise, and that highly
(not to speake it prophanely) that neyther having the accent
of Christians, nor the [gate] of Christian, Pagan, [or Norman],
have so strutted and bellowed, that I have thought some
of Natures Jouerney-men had made men, and not made
them well, they imitated Humanity so abhominably .

---

8   And let those that
play your Clownes, speake no more [then] is set downe for
them .

9   For there be of them, that will themselves laugh,
to set on some quantitie of barren Spectators to laugh
too, though in the meane time, some necessary Question
of the Play be [then] to be considered : that's Villanous, &
shewes a most pittifull Ambition in the Foole that uses it .

10 Go make you readie .

The speech is essentially composed of two parts, Hamlet's instructions to
the actors and his seemingly irrelevant digressions into his own reflections
upon and reactions to what he regards as "bad acting"—and although
commentators offer several contemporary explanations as to why, to sat-
isfy an audience, there still must be a theatrical reason to justify these dis-
tractions. F's orthography shows that whereas the instructions are mainly

intellectual, the sidebars are either emotional or passionate—the need to release seeming to be very important, perhaps suggesting his distress with all the bad real-life acting going on around him (Claudius, Rosincrance, Guildensterne, and even Ophelia).

• The importance of the forthcoming event is underscored by there being virtually no unembellished lines throughout the forty-one lines of advice and reminiscence until the very last words, F #10's "Go make you readie."

• The short F #3, "Pray you avoid it," is the other interesting exception, for both it and the very few surround phrases seem to go beyond just advice to the players, but reveal Hamlet's need for outward signs of honorable behavior from all around him:

> . Nor do not saw the Ayre too much [ ] your hand thus, but
> use all gently ;
> : I could have such a Fellow whipt for o're-doing Termagant :
> it out-Herod's Herod .
> : that's Villanous, & shewes a most pittifull Ambition in the
> Foole that uses it .

• The opening advice of "Speake the Speech" is strongly intellectual (F #1, 15/6), only to be broken by strong emotion as he becomes sidetracked into expressing at length what "offends mee to the Soule" (5/9, F #2's first four and a half lines), while the thought of whipping the "Fellow" who offends him becomes totally intellectual (4/0 in F #2's last two surround phrase line and a half)

• After the quiet imploring of the short F #3, as Hamlet returns to his series of instructions his passions return (F #4, 2/2), which he quickly reins in, reestablishing intellectual control (21/9, F #5–6) for the remainder of his instructions

• But once more, as he breaks off into describing bad actors whose performances have offended him, his intellect gives way, this time to passion (8/9, F #7)

• Commentators acknowledge that F #8–9 is a contemporary reference to the "Clownes" of his own company improvising too much, so it's hardly surprising that this moment is first emotional (1/3, F #8), then with the intellectual elaboration (3/1, F #9's first three and a half lines), quickly turning to passion in his final surround phrase denunciation (3/3, F #9's last line and half)

• And after all the verbiage and sidetracks, as the time grows near for the performance that Hamlet hopes will reveal all, at last Hamlet becomes quiet (the unembellished F #10)

BRIEF BACKGROUND TO THE FIRST FOLIO

Neil Freeman

The First Folio

The end of 1623 saw the publication of the justifiably famed First Folio (F1). The single volume, published in a run of approximately one thousand copies at the princely sum of one pound (a tremendous risk, considering that a single play would sell at no more than six pence, one-fortieth of F1's price, and that the annual salary of a schoolmaster was only ten pounds), contained thirty-six plays.

The manuscripts from which each F1 play would be printed came from a variety of sources. Some had already been printed. Some came from the playhouse complete with production details. Some had no theatrical input at all but were handsomely copied out and easy to read. Some were supposedly very messy, complete with first draft scribbles and crossings out. Yet, as Charlton Hinman, the revered dean of First Folio studies, describes F1 in the Introduction to the Norton Facsimile:

> It is of inestimable value for what it is, for what it contains. For here
> are preserved the masterworks of the man universally recognized
> as our greatest writer; and preserved, as Ben Jonson realized at the
> time of the original publication, not for an age but for all time.

What Does F1 Represent?

- texts prepared for actors who rehearsed three days for a new play and one day for one already in the repertoire
- written in a style (rhetoric incorporating debate) so different from ours (grammatical) that many modern alterations based on grammar (or poetry) have done remarkable harm to the rhetorical/debate quality of the original text and thus to interpretations of characters
- written for an acting company the core of which steadily grew older, and whose skills and interests changed markedly over twenty years as well as for an audience whose makeup and interests likewise changed as the company grew more experienced

The whole is based upon supposedly the best documents available at the time, collected by men closest to Shakespeare throughout his career, and brought to a single printing house whose errors are now widely understood—far more than those of some of the printing houses that produced the original quartos.

The Key Question

What text have you been working with—a good modern text or an "original" text, that is, a copy of one of the first printings of the play?

If it's a modern text, no matter how well edited, despite all the learned information offered, it's not surprising that you feel somewhat at a loss, for there is a huge difference between the original printings (the First Folio and the individual quartos) and any text prepared after 1700 right up to the most modern of editions. All the post-1700 texts have been tidied up for the modern reader to ingest silently, revamped according to the rules of correct grammar, syntax, and poetry. However, the "originals" were prepared for actors speaking aloud, playing characters often in a great deal of emotional and/or intellectual stress, and were set down on paper according to the very flexible rules of rhetoric and a seemingly very cavalier attitude toward the rules of grammar, and syntax, and spelling, and capitalization, and even poetry.

Unfortunately, because of the grammatical and syntactical standardization in place by the early 1700s, many of the quirks and oddities of the original also have been dismissed as "accidental"—usually as compositor error either in deciphering the original manuscript, falling prey to their own particular idiosyncrasies, or not having calculated correctly the amount of space needed to set the text. Modern texts dismiss the possibility that these very quirks and oddities may be by Shakespeare, hearing his characters in as much difficulty as poor Peter Quince is in *A Midsummer Night's Dream* (when he, as the Prologue, terrified and struck down by stage fright, makes a huge grammatical hash in introducing his play "Pyramus and Thisbe" before the aristocracy, whose acceptance or rejection can make or break him):

> If we offend, it is with our good will.
> That you should think, we come not to offend,
> But with good will.

> To show our simple skill,
> That is the true beginning of our end .
> Consider then, we come but in despite.
> We do not come, as minding to content you ,
> Our true intent is.
> > All for your delight
> We are not here.
> > That you should here repent you,
> The Actors are at hand; and by their show,
> You shall know all, that you are like to know.
>
> (*A Midsummer Night's Dream*)

In many other cases in the complete works what was originally printed is equally "peculiar," but, unlike Peter Quince, these peculiarities are usually regularized by most modern texts.

Most of these "peculiarities" resulted from Shakespeare setting down for his actors the stresses, trials, and tribulations the characters are experiencing as they think and speak, and thus are theatrical gold dust for the actor, director, scholar, teacher, and general reader alike.

The First Essential Difference between the Two Texts: Thinking

A **modern** text can show:

- the story line
- your character's conflict with the world at large
- your character's conflict with certain individuals within that world

but because of the very way an "original" text was set, it can show you all this plus one key extra, the very thing that makes big speeches what they are:

- the conflict within the character

Why?

Any good playwright writes about characters in stressful situations who are often in a state of conflict, not only with the world around them and the people in that world, but also within themselves. And you probably know from personal experience that when these conflicts occur, people do not necessarily utter the most perfect of grammatical/poetic/syntactic statements, phrases, or sentences. Joy and delight, pain and sorrow often come sweeping through in the way things are said, in the incoherence of the phrases, the running together of normally disassociated ideas, and even in the sounds of the words themselves.

The tremendous advantage of the period in which Shakespeare was setting his plays down on paper and how they first appeared in print was that when characters were rational and in control of self and situation, their phrasing and sentences (and poetic structure) would appear to be quite normal even to a modern eye—but when things were going wrong, these sentences and phrasing (and poetic structure) would become highly erratic. But the Quince-type eccentricities are rarely allowed to stand. Sadly, in tidying, most modern texts usually make the text far too clean, thus setting rationality when none originally existed.

The Second Essential Difference between First Folio and Modern Texts: Speaking, Arguing, Debating

Having discovered what and how you or your character is thinking is only the first stage of the work. You/the character then have to speak aloud, in a society that absolutely loved to speak—and not only speak ideas (content) but to speak entertainingly so as to keep listeners enthralled (and this was especially so when you have little content to offer and have to mask it somehow; think of today's television adverts and political spin doctors as a parallel, and you get the picture). Indeed one of the Elizabethan "how to win an argument" books was very precise about this: George Puttenham, *The Art of English Poesie* (1589).

ELIZABETHAN SCHOOLING

All educated classes could debate/argue at the drop of a hat, for both boys (in "petty-schools") and girls (by books and tutors) were trained in what was known overall as the art of rhetoric, which itself was split into three parts:

- First, how to distinguish the real from false appearances/outward show (think of the three caskets in *The Merchant of Venice* in which the language on the gold and silver caskets enticingly, and deceptively, seems to offer hopes of great personal rewards that are dashed when the language is carefully explored, whereas once the apparent threat on the lead casket is carefully analyzed, the reward therein is the greatest that could be hoped for).

- Second, how to frame your argument on one of "three great grounds": honor/morality; justice/legality; and, when all else fails, expedience/practicality.
- Third, how to order and phrase your argument so winsomely that your audience will vote for you no matter how good the opposition—and there were well over two hundred rules and variations by which winning could be achieved, all of which had to be assimilated before a child's education was considered over and done with.

THINKING ON YOUR FEET: THAT IS, THE QUICK, DEFT, RAPID MODIFICATION OF EACH TINY THOUGHT

The Elizabethan—therefore, your character, and therefore, you—was also trained to explore and modify thoughts as they spoke—never would you see a sentence in its entirety and have it perfectly worked out in your mind before you spoke (unless it was a deliberately written, formal public declaration, as with the Officer of the Court in *The Winter's Tale*, reading the charges against Hermione). Thus, after uttering your very first phrase, you might expand it, or modify it, deny it, change it, and so on throughout the whole sentence and speech.

From the poet Samuel Taylor Coleridge, there is a wonderful description of how Shakespeare put thoughts together like "a serpent twisting and untwisting in its own strength," that is, with one thought springing out of the one previous. Treat each new phrase as a fresh unraveling of the serpent's coil. What is discovered (and therefore said) is only revealed as the old coil/phrase disappears, revealing a new coil in its place. The new coil is the new thought. The old coil moves/disappears because the previous phrase is finished with as soon as it is spoken.

MODERN APPLICATION

It is very rarely that we speak dispassionately in our "real" lives. After all, thoughts give rise to feelings, feelings give rise to thoughts, and we usually speak both together—unless

1. we're trying very hard for some reason to control ourselves and not give ourselves away;

2. or the volcano of emotions within us is so strong that we cannot control ourselves, and feelings swamp thoughts;

3. and sometimes whether deliberately or unconsciously, we color words according to our feelings; the humanity behind the words so revealed is instantly understandable.

HOW THE ORIGINAL TEXTS NATURALLY ENHANCE/UNDERSCORE THIS CONTROL OR RELEASE

The amazing thing about the way all Elizabethan/early Jacobean texts were first set down (the term used to describe the printed words on the page being "orthography"), is that it was flexible, allowing for such variations to be automatically set down without fear of grammatical repercussion.

So if Shakespeare heard Juliet's Nurse working hard to try to convince Juliet that the Prince's nephew Juliet is being forced to (bigamously) marry, instead of setting the everyday normal

> O he's a lovely gentleman

which the modern texts HAVE to set, the first printings were permitted to set

> O hee's a Lovely Gentleman

suggesting that something might be going on inside the Nurse that causes her to release such excessive energy.

BE CAREFUL

This needs to be stressed very carefully: the orthography doesn't dictate to you/force you to accept exactly what it means. The orthography simply suggests that you might want to explore this moment further or more deeply.

In other words, simply because of the flexibility with which the Elizabethans/Shakespeare could set down on paper what they heard in their minds or wanted their listeners to hear, in addition to all the modern acting necessities of character—situation, objective, intention, action, and tactics—the original Shakespeare texts offer pointers to where feelings (either emotional or intellectual, or when combined together as passion, both) are also evident.

Summary

Basic Approach to First Folio Speeches on the Following Pages:

1. First, use the modern version shown first. By doing so you can discover:

- the basic plot line of what's happening to the character
- the first set of conflicts/obstacles impinging on the character as a result of the situation or actions of other characters
- the supposed grammatical and poetical correctnesses of the speech

2. Then you can explore:

- any acting techniques you'd apply to any modern soliloquy, including establishing for the character
- the given circumstances of the scene
- their outward state of being (who they are sociologically, etc.)
- their intentions and objectives
- the resultant action and tactics they decide to pursue

3. When this is complete, consult the First Folio version of the text. This will help you discover and explore:

- the precise thinking and debating process so essential to an understanding of any Shakespeare text
- the moments when the text is *not* grammatically or poetically as correct as the modern texts would have you believe, which will in turn help you recognize the moments of conflict and struggle stemming from within the character itself
- the sense of fun and enjoyment Shakespeare's language nearly always offers you no matter how dire the situation

Should you wish to further explore even more the differences between the two texts, the commentary that follows discusses how the First Folio has been changed and what those alterations might mean for the human arc of the speech.

Notes on How the First Folio Speeches Are Set Up

Each of the scenes that follow consists of the modern text with commentary, as well as select speeches from the First Folio, which will include the background on the speech and other information including number of lines, approximate timing, and who is addressed.

PROBABLE TIMING: Shown on the page before the speech begins. 0.45 = a forty-five-second speech

Symbols & Abbreviations in the Commentary and Text

F: the First Folio

mt.: modern texts

F # followed by a number: the number of the sentence under discussion in the First Folio version of the speech; thus F #7 would refer to the seventh sentence

mt. # followed by a number: the number of the sentence under discussion in the modern text version of the speech, thus mt. #5 would refer to the fifth sentence

/# (e.g., 3/7): the first number refers to the number of capital letters in the passage under discussion; the second refers to the number of long spellings therein

/ within a quotation from the speech, the "/" symbol indicates where one verse line ends and a fresh one starts

[ ] : set around words in both texts when F1 sets one word, mt another

{ } : some minor alteration has been made, in a speech built up, where a word or phrase will be changed, added, or removed

{†} : this symbol shows where a sizable part of the text is omitted

Terms Found in the Commentary

OVERALL

1. **orthography**: the capitalization, spellings, punctuation of the First Folio

SIGNS OF IMPORTANT DISCOVERIES/ARGUMENTS WITHIN A FIRST FOLIO SPEECH

2. **major punctuation**: colons and semicolons: since the Shakespeare texts are based so much on the art of debate and argument, the importance of F1's major punctuation must not be underestimated, for both the semicolon (;) and colon (:) mark a moment of importance for the character, either for itself, as a moment of discovery or revelation, or as a

key point in a discussion, argument, or debate that it wishes to impress upon other characters onstage.

As a rule of thumb:

a. the more frequent colon (:) suggests that whatever the power of the point discovered or argued, the character is not sidetracked and can continue with the argument—as such, the colon can be regarded as a **logical** connection

b. the far less frequent semicolon (;) suggests that because of the power inherent in the point discovered or argued, the character is sidetracked and momentarily loses the argument and falls back into itself or can only continue the argument with great difficulty—as such, the semicolon should be regarded as an **emotional** connection

3. **surround phrases**: phrase(s) surrounded by major punctuation, or a combination of major punctuation and the end or beginning of a sentence: thus these phrases seem to be of special importance for both character and speech, well worth exploring as key to the argument made and/or emotions released

A LOOSE RULE OF THUMB TO THE THINKING PROCESS OF A FIRST FOLIO CHARACTER

1. mental discipline/**intellect**: a section where capitals dominate suggests that the intellectual reasoning behind what is being spoken or discovered is of more concern than the personal response beneath it

2. feelings/**emotions**: a section where long spellings dominate suggests that the personal response to what is being spoken or discovered is of more concern than the intellectual reasoning behind it

3. **passion**: a section where both long spellings and capitals are present in almost equal proportions suggests that mind and emotion/feelings are inseparable, and thus the character is speaking passionately

SIGNS OF LESS THAN GRAMMATICAL THINKING WITHIN A FIRST FOLIO SPEECH

1. **onrush**: sometimes thoughts are coming so fast that several topics are joined together as one long sentence, suggesting that the F character's mind is working very quickly, or that his/her emotional state is causing some concern. Most modern texts split such a sentence into several grammatically correct parts (the opening speech of *As You Like It* is a

fine example, where F's long eighteen-line opening sentence is split into six), while the modern texts' resetting may be syntactically correct, the F moment is nowhere near as calm as the revisions suggest.

2. **fastlink**: sometimes F shows thoughts moving so quickly for a character that the connecting punctuation between disparate topics is merely a comma, suggesting that there is virtually no pause in springing from one idea to the next. Unfortunately, most modern texts rarely allow this to stand, instead replacing the obviously disturbed comma with a grammatical period, once more creating calm that it seems the original texts never intended to show.

FIRST FOLIO SIGNS OF WHEN VERBAL GAME PLAYING HAS TO STOP

1. **nonembellished**: a section with neither capitals nor long spellings suggests that what is being discovered or spoken is so important to the character that there is no time to guss it up with vocal or mental excesses: an unusual moment of self-control.

2. **short sentence**: coming out of a society where debate was second nature, many of Shakespeare's characters speak in long sentences in which ideas are stated, explored, redefined, and summarized, all before moving on to the next idea in the argument, discovery, or debate. The longer sentence is the sign of a rhetorically trained mind used to public speaking (oratory), but at times an idea or discovery is so startling or inevitable that length is either unnecessary or impossible to maintain: hence the occasional very important short sentence suggests that there is no time for the niceties of oratorical adornment with which to sugar the pill—verbal games are at an end, and now the basic core of the issue must be faced.

3. **monosyllabic**: with English being composed of two strands, the polysyllabic (stemming from French, Italian, Latin, and Greek), and the monosyllabic (from the Anglo-Saxon), each strand has two distinct functions: the polysyllabic words are often used when there is time for fanciful elaboration and rich description (which could be described as "excessive rhetoric") while the monosyllabic occur when, literally, there is no other way of putting a basic question or comment: Juliet's "Do you love me? I know thou wilt say aye" is a classic example of both monosyllables and non-embellishment. With monosyllables, only the naked truth is being spoken; nothing is hidden.

SCENE STUDY

Act II, Scene ii

Macbeth and Lady Macbeth

Macbeth has earlier this evening feasted Duncan, King of Scotland, at a banquet in his honor. After the King goes to bed, Macbeth kills him in his sleep.

Lady Macbeth is an accomplice; she has drugged the men who guard the King's bedchamber and urged her husband to be "so much more the man" by committing the murder which promises to make them King and Queen of Scotland. She had staked their marriage on his success:

> From this time
> Such I account thy love . . .   (I.vii.38–39)

and had shamed him into action with the assurance that she would have dashed out the brains of her own infant at her breast:

> had I so sworn as you
> Have done to this.   (I.vii.54–59)

Two daggers and some blood will be needed to perform this scene, and someone to knock at a door some distance offstage.

⊂⊃

Enter LADY MACBETH.

LADY MACBETH

> That which hath made them drunk hath made me bold;
> What hath quenched them hath given me fire. Hark!
>   Peace!
> It was the owl that shrieked, the fatal bellman
> Which gives the stern'st good-night. He is about it.

3   **bellman** (the owl, bird of death,   to warn a condemned prisoner the
    is compared to the bellman sent   night before his execution)

The doors are open and the surfeited grooms   5
Do mock their charge with snores. I have drugged their possets,
    their possets,
That death and nature do contend about them
Whether they live or die.

MACBETH   *(Within.)* Who's there? What ho?

LADY MACBETH

Alack, I am afraid they have awaked
And 'tis not done! Th' attempt and not the deed   10
Confounds us. Hark! I laid their daggers ready;
He could not miss 'em. Had he not resembled
My father as he slept, I had done't.

    Enter MACBETH.

LADY MACBETH   My husband!

MACBETH

    I have done the deed. Didst thou not hear a noise?

LADY MACBETH

    I heard the owl scream and the crickets cry.   15
    Did not you speak?

MACBETH   When?

LADY MACBETH   Now.

MACBETH   As I descended?

LADY MACBETH Ay.

MACBETH Hark!
    Who lies i' th' second chamber?

LADY MACBETH   Donalbain.

MACBETH This is a sorry sight.   20

---

  5 **grooms** household servants

  6 **mock . . . snores** make a mockery of their duty to guard the king by sleeping
    possets bed-time drinks

  7 **nature** natural life

  11 **Confounds** destroys

  20 **sorry** painful/wretched, worthless

LADY MACBETH

A foolish thought, to say a sorry sight.

MACBETH

There's one did laugh in's sleep and one cried "Murder!"

That they did wake each other. I stood and heard them.

But they did say their prayers and addressed them

Again to sleep.

LADY MACBETH There are two lodged together.   25

MACBETH

One cried "God bless us!" and "Amen" the other,

As they had seen me with these hangman's hands.

List'ning their fear, I could not say "Amen,"

When they did say "God bless us!"

LADY MACBETH   Consider it not so deeply.

MACBETH

But wherefore could not I pronounce "Amen"?   30

I had most need of blessing and "Amen"

Stuck in my throat.

LADY MACBETH These deeds must not be thought

After these ways; so it will make us mad.

MACBETH

Methought I heard a voice cry "Sleep no more!

Macbeth does murder sleep"—the innocent sleep,   35

Sleep that knits up the raveled sleave of care,

The death of each day's life, sore labor's bath,

Balm of hurt minds, great nature's second course,

Chief nourisher in life's feast.

LADY MACBETH   What do you mean?

27 **hangman's** i.e., bloody (he dis
    membered as well as hanged)

36 **raveled sleave** tangled skein

38 **course** dish (in a feast)/way of
    living (compared with waking life)

MACBETH

Still it cried "Sleep no more!" to all the house: 40
"Glamis hath murdered sleep and therefore Cawdor
Shall sleep no more: Macbeth shall sleep no more."

LADY MACBETH

Who was it that thus cried? Why, worthy thane,
You do unbend your noble strength, to think
So brainsickly of things. Go get some water   45
And wash this filthy witness from your hand.
Why did you bring these daggers from the place?
They must lie there: go carry them and smear
The sleepy grooms with blood.

MACBETH   I'll go no more.

I am afraid to think what I have done;   50
Look on't again I dare not.

LADY MACBETH   Infirm of purpose!

Give me the daggers. The sleeping and the dead
Are but as pictures. 'Tis the eye of childhood
That fears a painted devil. If he do bleed,
I'll gild the faces of the grooms withal   55
For it must seem their guilt.   *Exit. Knock within.*

MACBETH   Whence is that knocking?

How is't with me when every noise appalls me?
What hands are here? Ha, they pluck out mine eyes!
Will all great Neptune's ocean wash this blood
Clean from my hand? No, this my hand will rather   60
The multitudinous seas incarnadine,
Making the green one red.

Enter LADY MACBETH.

44	**unbend** undo (unstring a bow)	55	**gild** paint
46	**witness** evidence	61	**incarnadine** redden
54	**painted** i.e., unreal	62	**green one** i.e., the ocean

LADY MACBETH

My hands are of your color but I shame

To wear a heart so white. *(Knock.)* I hear a knocking

At the south entry. Retire we to our chamber.   65

A little water clears us of this deed:

How easy is it then! Your constancy

Hath left you unattended. Hark! More

knocking.

Get on your nightgown, lest occasion call us

And show us to be watchers. Be not lost   70

So poorly in your thoughts.

MACBETH

To know my deed, 'twere best not know myself.

(Knock.)

Wake Duncan with thy knocking! I would thou

couldst!   *Exeunt.*

67	**constancy** fortitude, faithfulness	70	**watchers** i.e., awake late
68	**left you unattended** deserted you	71	**poorly** unworthily
69	**nightgown** dressing gown	72	**To . . .myself** i.e., having done what I have done, I had rather not be myself

ՀՅՑՀ

Rehearsing the Scene

This scene should be played as if in near-darkness. One or both of the characters might carry a light. The scene is set after everyone has gone to bed, so Lady Macbeth should be dressed ready for bed, but Macbeth is fully clothed. Macbeth's cry from offstage should be strained or indistinct so that his wife's elation changes at once to fear. She sees again, in her mind's eye, the old King lying asleep at the scene of the crime. The impact of the murder is so powerful that it goes beyond Duncan's death to a vision of her own father: "Had he not resembled my father."

Is she voicing her compassion or her horror? Or self-reproach for not being able to commit the crime herself? All her words have seemed to come involuntarily, but these must have sufficient compulsion or purpose to obliterate other concerns about the details of the plot. Then, at this very moment, Macbeth enters with bloody hands, holding two daggers. She turns to him and, either involuntarily or with careful reassurance, says simply, "My husband."

This opening sets the level and tone for the whole scene: it is alive with immediate awareness; sharp with wordplay and double-think which reach out to hold violent images in place; and quick with shifting feelings which, in a brief moment, can send consciousness lurching forward or backward in time, and reaching upward or plummeting down to other modes of consciousness.

Actors must be patient in unraveling the movements within these characters' consciousnesses. The scene is rich with clues to physical actions which reveal the characters' inner struggles. For example, neither of them mentions the blood on Macbeth's hands until line 20. Does Lady Macbeth notice it before then? What is it which awakens Macbeth's consciousness to speak of the "sorry sight"—but not to speak of the blood itself until line 27? Why does Macbeth fasten on the simple prayer, belonging to ordinary and peaceful existence, in much the same way as Lady Macbeth remembered the image of her father? Why does he repeat the simple words, even though they torture him? While his wife recalls him to practical business, why does Macbeth become haunted by fantasy and then by a lingering memory of the blessings of gentle sleep? When he, like an unstringed bow (see l. 44), stands "brainsick" and perhaps almost "mad" (ll. 45 and 33), Lady Macbeth takes the initiative, her hands clutching the daggers and so becoming red like his: is her action carefully considered or impulsive? Does she remember the "eye of childhood" because he is so obviously terrified of the blood, or to reassure herself?

At line 56 a knock is heard from some distance off stage. This intrusive sound almost represents another character, at least a reminder of a world other than the nightmarish one which they both inhabit. The sound quickens Macbeth's private horror; it "appalls" him (l. 57). He sees the blood on his hands again, but now as if those hands belong to someone else and are about to attack him. Then, with an extended, dreamlike image, his words ring out with an impulse that seems both to engulf and strengthen him. After a brief silence, Lady Macbeth reenters, reproves him and, when repeated knockings signal danger, gathers strength.

These characters live in the distant past, in the moment just past, in the burning, terrifying present, and in the future. Depending on how they have travelled on their individual journeys through the scene, meeting on the way only for brief and intense passages, they will leave the stage together or separately. She may support him, leading him; so his final words, as he begins to move off, are a confession of guilt after he has relinquished initiative to his wife. Or she may have to draw him, almost pull him, offstage, so that his last words are a defiance of her as well as the cry of a defeated man. Or he may now accept his own guilt and grief, using these words as a way of resisting his wife's judgment. In this case they may leave at the same time, but in distinctly different ways; he asserts his own sense of doom, she deals with practical and tangible matters. He may, however, leave before she does, hurrying at the sound of the knocking and paying little or no heed to what she has said. He may have become more frenzied and a little mad. Although she manages to cope with the situation, is there something in her assurance that all is "easy" (l. 67) which shows that she is also dealing with thoughts which threaten her sanity so that she overstates her case recklessly?

Although no one is present with them on stage, both characters are aware of others offstage, and both know that they must leave as soon as possible. The scene should therefore drive forward, even though actors may want to speak slowly and may choose sometimes to speak in a half-whisper. There are very few half verse lines to indicate pauses, except at the initial meeting when they listen in silence to know whether they are overheard or likely to be discovered. From this moment on, they follow close on each other's words, no matter how dissimilar their intentions or their thoughts.

First Folio Speeches

For another perspective, following are speeches from the scene from the First Folio with commentary by Neil Freeman drawn from the *Once More Unto the Speech* series. The First Folio used abbreviations not familiar today—e.g., in the first line where the ¨ symbol indicates a dropped letter in the word "thee" ("thë").

LADY   THAT WHICH HATH MADE THË DRUNK, HATH MADE ME BOLD :

Background: Lady Macbeth awaits her husband's return from killing Duncan and lays the blame on his "spungie Officers," currently in a drug-induced sleep, by leaving the incriminating blood-stained daggers by their hands.

Style: solo

Where: the castle at Inverness, probably the battlements

To Whom: self and the audience

# of Lines: 14   **Probable Timing:** 0.45 minutes

Lady

1   That which hath made [thë] drunk, hath made me bold :
    What hath quench'd them, hath given me fire .

2   Hearke, peace : it was the Owle that shriek'd,
    The fatall Bell-man, which gives the stern'st good-night .

3   He is about it, the Doores are open :
    And the surfeted Groomes doe mock their charge
    With Snores .

4   I have drugg'd their Possets,
    That Death and Nature doe contend about them,
    Whether they live, or dye .

    ─────────────────────────────────────

5   Alack, I am afraid they have awak'd,
    And 'tis not done : th'attempt, and not the deed,

Confounds us : hearke : I lay'd their Daggers ready,

He could not misse 'em .

6   Had he not resembled

My Father as he slept, I had don't .

In the first two lines of this speech Macbeth's Lady tells us that she has been drinking, that she is "bold" and has "fire": following F's first line come six irregular ones (8 or 9/8/11/9 or 10/10/8 syllables) and these, plus F #2's onrush, suggest that she is finding it very difficult to keep an even balance: most modern texts remove both hints by restructuring the shaded passage to five lines as shown (10 or 11/11/11/10 or 11/12 syllables) and splitting F #3 into three.

- Whatever the effects of the drink, she starts very quietly (afraid others will overhear, perhaps) but with great conviction, with F #1 being triply weighted as two unembellished and almost monosyllabic surround phrases.

- Her determination to stay in control continues, with four more consecutive surround phrases, but the calm is now swept aside by passion: the onrushed F #2 (2/3) dealing with her being startled by the owl-cry and F #3 (3/3) dealing with her envisioning Macbeth about to strike.

- The passion continues, though without the extra intensity of surround phrases, as she dwells on how she has played her part by having drugged their drinks (F #4, 3/2).

- But (as the text suggests) a noise disturbs her and, as with the opening, she returns to five consecutive surround phrases, the fear of the first three heightened by being unembellished, as if she can barely voice the thoughts—

> . Alack, I am afraid they have awak'd, /
> And 'tis not done : th'attempt, and not the deed, /
> Confounds us :

—while perhaps another noise triggers the emotion (1/3) of the two that follow: ": hearke : I lay'd their Daggers ready, / He could not misse 'em ."

- Thus the quiet intellect of her last statement that it's only Duncan's resemblance to her father that has prevented her from killing him herself (F #6, 1/0) is thrown into even more relief as something very key to her inner workings.

LADY MY HANDS ARE OF YOUR COLOUR : BUT I SHAME /
TO WEARE A HEART SO WHITE .

Background: Macbeth has killed Duncan. However, he has failed to incriminate the guards as planned. The reasons? He heard a "voyce cry, Sleep no more" which, together with his inability to "say Amen" when the two guards "did say God blesse us" after their laughing or crying " "Murther" in their sleep, has prevented him from further rational behavior, to the extent of bringing the murder weapons back down with him. Thus his wife has had to take the daggers and place them beside the guards, which triggers the following as she returns.

Style: as part of a two-handed scene

Where: the castle at Inverness, probably the battlements

To Whom: her husband

# of Lines: 10   **Probable Timing:** 0.35 minutes

Lady

1   My Hands are of your colour : but I shame
    To weare a Heart so white .

[Knocke]

2   I heare a knocking at the South entry :
    Retyre we to our Chamber :
    A little Water cleares us of this deed .

3   How easie is it then ? your Constancie
    Hath left you unattended .

[Knocke]

4   Hearke, more knocking .

5   Get on your Night-Gowne, least occasion call us,
    And shew us to be Watchers : be not lost
    So poorely in your thoughts .

The temptation in such a short speech with such driving circumstances is to play the overall excitement/emotion as one generalized urging. However, F's orthography suggests that the speech falls into three distinct parts, a passionate opening and closing (F #1–2, and F #5), and a central portion that is far more reasoned and controlled—suggesting an attempt at reasoning which doesn't necessarily succeed. One note: the pauses inherent the F only short lines ending F #2 and between F #3–4 (indicated as shaded text) show where she offers Macbeth a chance to respond and he doesn't—which could well explain her increasing sense of frustration as well as the need for her to switch tactics twice in a very short speech.

• The passion of F #1, showing him Duncan's blood (2/2), and of F #2, the attempt to quickly wash the blood off of both of them so that they can face whoever's knocking without fear of discovery (3/3), is heightened by being set as five consecutive surround phrases.

• And though two more consecutive surround phrases and then a short sentence follow in her attempt to get him to comply (F #3–4, 1/1), she becomes very quiet—as if she were coaxing rather than scolding or verbally abusing him.

• Then, with no apparent response, her surround-phrase passion sweeps in once more as she attempts to move him to action (F #5, 3/2, all but the last phrase), while at the very last moment her emotion gets the better of her (0/1) as she orders/pleads with him via the surround phrase " : be not lost / So poorely in your thoughts . "

SCENE STUDY

Act III, Scene ii

Macbeth and Lady Macbeth

It is late in the day and Lady Macbeth has sent to tell her husband that she attends his "leisure" for a few words. But as soon as she is alone she speaks.

Together they have killed Duncan, King of Scotland, making it seem that his servants had been responsible. Macbeth has in turn killed the servants. The king's two sons have fled the land, and Macbeth has been "named" and "invested" as king (II.iv.31–32).

When all the thanes were called to a "solemn supper" (III.i.11–15) to celebrate the accession, Banquo was prepared to leave court with his son and so Macbeth had questioned his intentions. Banquo is his most dangerous rival: the witches who had prophesied that he would be king had also told Banquo that he would be "greater" and "more happy" than Macbeth: "Thou shalt get kings, though thou be none" (I.iii.64–66)

As Banquo rode from court promising to return for the feast in the evening, Macbeth had arranged to assassinate him and his son. Lady Macbeth does not know that he has done this.

☙❧

LADY MACBETH   Nought's had, all's spent,
  Where our desire is got without content.
  'Tis safer to be that which we destroy
  Than by destruction dwell in doubtful joy.

Enter MACBETH.

  How now, my lord! Why do you keep alone,   5

1 **Nought's . . . spent** i.e., we have achieved nothing and spent everything

4 **doubtful** apprehensive, fearful/ uncertain

Of sorriest fancies your companions making,

Using those thoughts which should indeed have died

With them they think on? Things without all remedy

Should be without regard: what's done is done.

MACBETH

We have scorched the snake, not killed it: 10

She'll close and be herself, whilst our poor malice

Remains in danger of her former tooth.

But let the frame of things disjoint, both the worlds suffer,

Ere we will eat our meal in fear and sleep

In the affliction of these terrible dreams   15

That shake us nightly. Better be with the dead,

Whom we, to gain our peace, have sent to peace,

Than on the torture of the mind to lie

In restless ecstasy. Duncan is in his grave;

After life's fitful fever he sleeps well.   20

Treason has done his worst: nor steel, nor poison,

Malice domestic, foreign levy, nothing,

Can touch him further.

LADY MACBETH   Come on,

Gentle my lord, sleek o'er your rugged looks;

6   **sorriest** most wretched
7   **Using** being familiar with
8   **without** beyond the reach of
10 **scorched** slashed (with a knife)
11 **close** heal
    malice power to do harm
12 **former tooth** i.e., her fangs, as dangerous as before
13 **frame . . . disjoint** structure of the universe falls apart
    both the worlds terrestrial and celestial worlds, heaven and earth
    suffer perish

17 **to gain . . . to peace** to put our minds at peace, have sent to the peace of death
18 **torture of the mind** (the bed is a rack, an instrument of torture)
19 **restless ecstasy** sleepless/unceasing frenzy, delirium
20 **fitful** violent, full of fits
21 **his** its
22 **Malice domestic** civil war
    levy army
23 **touch** wound
24 **sleek** smooth
    rugged furrowed, harsh

Be bright and jovial among your guests tonight.   25

MACBETH

So shall I, love; and so I pray be you:

Let your remembrance apply to Banquo,

Present him eminence both with eye and tongue.

Unsafe the while that we

Must lave our honors in these flattering streams   30

And make our faces vizards to our hearts,

Disguising what they are.

LADY MACBETH   You must leave this.

MACBETH

O full of scorpions is my mind, dear wife!

Thou know'st that Banquo and his Fleance lives.

LADY MACBETH

But in them nature's copy's not eterne.   35

MACBETH

There's comfort yet! They are assailable.

Then be thou jocund: ere the bat hath flown

His cloistered flight, ere to black Hecate's summons

The shard-borne beetle with his drowsy hums

Hath run night's yawning peal, there shall be done   40

A deed of dreadful note.

LADY MACBETH   What's to be done?

27	**apply** attend
28	**Present him eminence** pay him special honor
29–30	**Unsafe . . . streams** we are so in secure at this time that we clean (ironic) our royal dignities with endless flattery
31	**vizards** masks
33	**scorpions** (the sting of this reptile was proverbially intensely painful; also = whips, used as instruments of torture)

35	**copy** form/lease
	eterne eternal
38	**cloistered** (bats fly in and around buildings, rather than in open spaces)
	Hecate's summons (the Greek goddess commanded witches and presided over magical rites)
39	**shard-borne** born in dung, borne in the air by its wing-cases

MACBETH

> Be innocent of the knowledge, dearest chuck,
>
> Till thou applaud the deed. Come, seeling night,
>
> Scarf up the tender eye of pitiful day
>
> And with thy bloody and invisible hand   45
>
> Cancel and tear to pieces that great bond
>
> Which keeps me pale! Light thickens and the crow
>
> Makes wing to th' rooky wood.
>
> Good things of day begin to droop and drowse
>
> Whiles night's black agents to their preys do rouse.   50
>
> Thou marvel'st at my words. But hold thee still:
>
> Things bad begun make strong themselves by ill.
>
> So prithee, go with me.   *Exeunt.*

46 **bond** bond (in the natural order) of life/moral law

47 **pale** pale with fear
thickens grows dense, darkens

48 **rooky** i.e., black and filled with rooks

50 **to their . . . rouse** wake and rise up to start hunting

51 **hold thee still** keep constant, maintain your resolve

CR꙰CO

Rehearsing the Scene

Lady Macbeth's opening soliloquy reveals her inner restlessness, but as her husband enters she turns at once to tell him not to dwell on his secret thoughts. In answer he expresses the torture they both feel, reestablishing the "we" which his wife had used before he entered. Without having heard her words, he echoes her envy of Duncan, elaborating it, but remembers the possibility of "peace" rather than "content" (ll. 2 and 17). The incomplete verse-line 23 indicates a pause or silence before Lady Macbeth draws him toward practical business and his next task, offering neither comfort nor reproof for what he has just said. Now he can agree very simply and, by calling her "love," he seems to recognize her power to help him escape from their mutual fears.

For a moment Macbeth talks like she does, with pretended good humor and good heart, but a bitter and dark irony enters his speech which she at once detects: "You must leave this" (l. 32). He has not directly contradicted her, but she has no need to name the self-torture she rebukes and seeks to avoid; they understand each other completely. They could hold each other in their arms here. Macbeth now calls her "dear wife" (l. 33) and, pretending to good spirits, speaks directly of the pain in his heart.

Now the scene develops in a new direction. Indirectly he begins to talk of the next murder he has already set in motion. His wife seems to understand his intention or else suggests he should do what he has already done. Macbeth's spirits rise and he encourages her to be "jocund"—a word, in Shakespeare's plays, more carefree than her "bright and jovial" (l. 25). For example:

> As gentle and as jocund as to jest
> Go I to fight.   (*Richard II*, I.iii.95–96)

> The jocund day
> Stands tiptoe on the misty mountain tops . . .
>   (*Romeo and Juliet*, III.v.9–10)

But Macbeth's thoughts for himself are different. He becomes immersed in quite different visions; and he is strengthened by them too. Marvelously detailed and sensitive, his evocation of the planned assassination of Banquo and Fleance is dark, quiet and mysterious, like the coming of night in the natural world. Lady Macbeth asks only the simplest question now (l. 41), and this prompts him to protect her and to use his most intimate and contented way of addressing her— "dearest chuck." But then he turns away, summoning the night as if he were more powerful than Hecate, becoming at one with predatory and annihilating forces.

Perhaps some wordless response to the horror should come from Lady Macbeth which calls for his "Thou marvel'st at my words" (l. 51). But he may associate instinctively with her fears, without prompting, because he needs her to "hold" with him constantly. Perhaps his acceptance of "Things bad begun make strong themselves by ill" is linked by rhyme to his admonition of his wife to show that it is accompanied by a movement toward her, so that he seems to be made "strong" by her, as well as by his own committal to darkness and blood. Or does "So prithee, go with me" indicate that he knows that unless she is called to follow she will not do so? Does he fear that he has moved so far into "ill" that he will now have to act alone?

Macbeth is notoriously full of action and spectacle, but the action of this scene is what happens when the two protagonists meet. Macbeth enters because his wife has asked for him. He leaves the stage after he has asked her to go with him. The strongest and most significant action is within the two characters, their individual grappling with uncertainty, isolation, guilt, a need for peace and, perhaps in Macbeth only, a need for pride. Although it is possible to play the scene without them touching each other, they influence each other constantly, their relation ship changing with the interplay. This is why the writing is so dense, needing many annotations and patient study to follow its double meanings, fine distinctions, and multiple associations. The action is within these two characters, underneath what they say and fired partly by their sense of each other's presence.

Actors will find the words difficult to master until their characters' basic and inner actions begin to become clear to them. Yet the characters are implicit in those very words. The study process must develop in two ways: searching the words for clues to character; and using the action of being together to explore and establish each character's reality.

It may be helpful to ask which is the most important, most crucial and necessary, action for each character. 1) He protects his wife from knowledge of his new crime. He identifies himself with darkness, the witches, blood and evil. He denies the truth of "what's done is done." He sees life as a "fever," full of madness and violence. He realizes he would rather be dead than be uncertain and alive. 2) She tells her husband to pay no attention to what has been done and reminds him of what can be done. She senses that Macbeth cannot throw off his fears and so she suggests that these feelings may die if his rivals die. (She does not remind him of the witches' prophesy, but she dares to look to the future and so may arouse his thoughts of them so that they surface in the mention of Hecate.) She makes equal cause with him, speaking more directly and simply about what must be done. That is her last word, but not her last response: she may, indeed, "marvel" at his words (l. 52), regaining his attention al though remaining silent. She may respond to "Hold thee still" and certainly she must respond to his request that she should go with him. She is necessary to him, in some way; and Shakespeare's handling of the scene insists that she responds to this.

For Macbeth, the culmination of this scene is sustained with words, but for Lady Macbeth, when attention is brought to bear finally on her, there is not a single word to say. Her silent movement across the stage, choosing either to go with him, as he goes, or to move in her own time and with her own purpose, marks the conclusion of the scene. She has to be what she is: is this her most important action? For the silent movement to be fully expressive, she must have responded in her mind and body to every word Macbeth has spoken. Is it an act of courage, of love, of committal to violence, of despair, of defeat? Whatever the actress finds herself able to make this exit express, it will gain closest possible attention by contrast to the many words given to Macbeth at the close of the scene.

First Folio Speech

For another perspective, following is the speech from the scene from the First Folio with commentary by Neil Freeman drawn from the *Once More Unto the Speech* series.

MACBETH   WE HAVE SCORCH'D THE SNAKE, NOT KILL'D IT :

Background: For a while Macbeth has kept himself apart from his wife, not letting her in on any of his thoughts or plans. She finally confronts him, challenging him especially over his brooding—

> why doe you keepe alone? /
> Of sorryest Fancies your companions making, /
> Using those Thoughts, which should indeed have dy'd /
> With them they thinke on: things without all remedie /
> Should be without regard: what's done, is done

—which triggers the not particularly useful (to her) or logical reply. Her simple and firm rejection of this speech ("You must leave this") leads to the even more obscure ending ("O, full of Scorpions is my Minde, deare Wife"), which could be added here as a possible start to the speech. (No wonder she eventually "marvell'st" at the final speech in the scene—not set here—so full is it of the dark images associated with witchcraft and black magic.)

Style: both as part of a two-handed scene

Where: unspecified, but probably their private chambers at Scone

To Whom: Lady Macbeth

# of Lines: 15   **Probable Timing:** 0.50 minutes

Macbeth

1   We have [scorch'd] the Snake, not kill'd it :
    Shee'le close, and be her selfe, whilest our poore Mallice
    Remaines in danger of her former Tooth .

2   But let the frame of things dis-joynt,
    Both the Worlds suffer,
    Ere we will eate our Meale in feare, and sleepe

In the affliction of these terrible Dreames,

That shake us Nightly : Better be with the dead,

Whom we, to gayne our peace, have sent to peace,

[Then] on the torture of the Minde to lye

In restlesse extasie .

3   Duncane is in his Grave :

After Lifes fitfull Fever, he sleepes well,

Treason ha's done his worst : nor Steele, nor Poyson,

Mallice domestique, forraine Levie, nothing,

Can touch him further .

As Macbeth utters the appalling thoughts of allowing the order of both the natural and the magical world to "dis-joynt" (the start of F #2) and that life is "fitful" and perhaps death is welcome (the link between F #2 and F #3), F emphasizes the struggle within him by setting two sets of short lines (8/5 syllables and 6/6 syllables respectively). The tiny pauses thus created allow him moments to regain self-control: most modern texts reset both as single lines, longer than iambic pentameter (13 and 12 syllables respectively), thus substituting F's pause with an onrush instead.

• The depth of the problem shared by both Macbeth and his wife is intensified via the opening surround phrase " . We have scorch'd the Snake, not kill'd it : " and F #1's subsequent emotions (3/6).

• But after the passionate split-line avowal that he is prepared to let "the frame of things dis-joynt" (1/1), F #2's fleshing out of the horrors he is now undergoing through lack of sleep, he returns to emotions once more (5/9) . . .

• . . . while the strange passionate thoughts (F #3, 6/8) which seem to be created by his inability to sleep are also heightened with surround phrases:

> " . Duncane is in his Grave : /
> After Lifes fitfull Fever, he sleepes well, /
> Treason ha's done his worst : "

WORKING WITH MODERN AND
FIRST FOLIO TEXTS

It is important when working on text that you gain information from modern edited texts, such as the Applause Shakespeare Library, which can provide much information on understanding what is happening in the scene, and then look at the original printed texts of the First Folio, such as the Applause First Folio Editions, which can give additional insights.

So on the pages that follow, we look at several of the key speeches in the play, including the Captain's report from the battlefield, Lady Macbeth's ruminations after reading the latter from her husband, and husband and wife in I.vii confronting the prospect of Duncan's murder. We first look at these speeches as they appear in the Applause Shakespeare Library and then as rendered in *Once More Unto the Speech* by Neil Freeman.

We are often unaware of how many changes have been made by editors in the effort to standardize Shakespeare. For example, several lines in the Captain's speech that are halting and irregular in the original Folio are set in a more conventional pentameter in many modern editions. Another significant change is that in modern texts the role of Macbeth's wife is typically given as "Lady Macbeth," whereas in the First Folio she is merely "Lady."

Captain's Speech, I.ii: Modern Text

Alarum°   within. Enter KING [DUNCAN], MALCOLM, DON-
ALBAIN, LENNOX, with attendants, meeting a bleeding CAPTAIN.

DUNCAN What bloody man is that? He can report,
As seemeth by his plight, of the revolt
The newest state.
MALCOLM   This is the sergeant,°
Who, like a good and hardy soldier, fought
'Gainst my captivity—hail, brave friend!   5
Say to the King the knowledge of the broil°
As thou didst leave it.
CAPTAIN   Doubtful it stood,
As two spent swimmers that do cling together
And choke their art. The merciless Macdonwald
(Worthy to be a rebel, for to that°   10
The multiplying villanies of nature
Do swarm upon him) from the Western Isles°
Of kerns and gallowglasses°   is supplied,
And Fortune, on his damned quarrel smiling,
Showed like a rebel's whore.°   But all's too weak,   15
For brave Macbeth (well he deserves that name°   ),
Disdaining Fortune, with his brandished steel,
Which smoked°   with bloody execution,
Like valor's minion,°   carved out his passage,
Till he faced the slave;   20
Which°   ne'er shook hands, nor bade farewell to him,
Till he unseamed him from the nave to th' chops,°
And fixed his head upon our battlements.
DUNCAN O valiant cousin, worthy gentleman!
CAPTAIN As whence the sun 'gins his reflection,°   25
Shipwracking storms and direful°   thunders break,
So from that springe°   whence comfort seemed to come,
Discomfort swells. Mark, King of Scotland, mark:
No sooner justice had, with valor armed,
Compelled these skipping kerns to trust their heels,   30
But the Norweyan lord,°   surveying vantage,°
With furbished°   arms, and new supplies of men,
Began a fresh assault.

alarm

ranking officer

battle

i.e., to that end
Hebrides and Ireland,
    west of Scotland
light- and heavy-armed
    Irish foot-soldiers

seemed to prostitute
    herself for a rebel
i.e., of a "brave" man
steamed
favorite

who (i.e., Macbeth)
navel to the jaws

begins to turn back (from
    movement south in
    winter)
dreadful
1. season; 2. source

Sweno   seeing his
    opportunity
fresh

1–7   The Folio's "Alarums within" requires sounds of battle to take over from the sounds of storm in the opening scene. If the witches have dispersed by three separate routes, Duncan's entry, fully attended, will draw attention to one side of the stage, so that the "bleeding Captain" will not be seen as he enters, but appear unannounced to take the place of the mysterious witches. So, before he speaks, he can give an impression of fateful timing (the witches had spoken of a battle in progress). Is he Macbeth, whom they had announced? Is he another apparition? Duncan's first words indicate that he stands at first at some distance from the royal entourage.

7–45   As soon as the Captain speaks, it is clear that he brings a tale of bloodshed, not news of a victory. (The battle is not yet "lost and won," the sun not yet "set"; see I.i.4–5.) He supplies more than exposition: ornate figures of speech give a studied or "held" effect, while parentheses, unusual word order and some abrupt phrases, together with the rhythms of the speech, add urgency and, perhaps, an impression of a continuous struggle for fit expression. Several times he is carried away by his own tale and lives in the exciting past, using the present tense. Reference to "direful thunders" and the opposition of "comfort'" and "discomfort'" (ll. 27–28) may be heard by the audience as eerie echoes of the previous scene, especially the riddle-like "fair is foul." Short verse lines suggest pauses, for breath rather than rhetorical effect; at line 42, his "report'" finished, the Captain is in so much pain that his physical distress is as impressive as anything he has said.

Duncan's responses ensure that Macbeth, although still not seen by the audience, remains an empowering force in this scene, as he was the main interest of the previous one. The king's ecstatic praise for Macbeth's amazing physical feat (l. 24)—slicing his adversary in two, from the groin to the head, with one rising stroke of his sword—shows that such butchery is admired and a sign of honor in Duncan's kingdom. Is Scotland to be portrayed as especially

DUNCAN   Dismayed not this
Our captains, Macbeth and Banquo?
CAPTAIN   Yes,
As sparrows eagles, or the hare the lion.   35
If I say sooth,° I must report they were
As cannons° overcharged with double cracks,
So they
Doubly redoubled strokes upon the foe—
Except they meant to bathe in reeking wounds,   40
Or memorize° another Golgotha,°
I cannot tell—
But I am faint, my gashes cry for help.
DUNCAN So well thy words become thee, as thy wounds;
They smack of honor both. Go, get him surgeons.   45
[*Exit* CAPTAIN, *escorted by attendants.*]

speak truth
(an anachronism; cannons
   were not used until the
   14th century)

make famous   place
   of skulls where Christ
   was crucified (Matthew
   27:33)

barbaric? Is Duncan a king who wishes to use violence, but is dependent on others to do this for him? Sometimes Duncan is played as a holy and sainted king, but such a reading of the part, and of the play, is hard to reconcile with his sentiments here unless evil is thought to justify a relish of brutality. In Trevor Nunn's 1976 production, Duncan was "very infirm . . . dressed in white and accompanied by church organ music" (Shakespeare Survey, 30).

Captain's Speech, I.ii: First Folio Text

CAPTAINE   DOUBTFULL IT STOOD, / AS TWO SPENT
SWIMMERS, THAT DOE CLING TOGETHER, I.II.7–42

Background: The injured Captain (called the "Serjeant" by Malcome, and named as such in some modern texts) reports on the most recent battle in the civil war. One note: the Scottish rebels are being aided by foreign powers, hence the reference to "Westerne Isles" (of Scotland) and "the Norweyan Lord."

Style: one-on-one address for the benefit of the group as a whole
Where: close to the battlefield
To Whom: King Duncan, with his sons Malcome and Donalbaine, Lenox, and "attendants"
# of Lines: 35   **Probable Timing:** 1.45 minutes

Captaine

1   Doubtfull it stood,
     As two spent Swimmers, that doe cling together,
     And choake their Art : The mercilesse Macdonwald
     (Worthie to be a Rebell, for to that
     The multiplying Villanies of Nature
     Doe swarme upon him) from the Westerne Isles
     Of Kernes and [Gallowgrosses] is supply'd,
     And Fortune on his damned [Quarry] smiling,
     Shew'd like a Rebells Whore : but all's too weake :
     For brave Macbeth (well hee deserves that Name)
     Disdayning Fortune, with his brandisht Steele,
     Which smoak'd with bloody execution
     (Like Valours Minion) carv'd out his passage,
     Till hee fac'd the Slave :
     Which nev'r shooke hands, nor bad farwell to him,
     Till he unseam'd him from the Nave toth' Chops,
     And fix'd his Head upon our Battlements .

     _____

2   As whence the Sunne 'gins his reflection,
     Shipwracking Stormes, and direfull Thunders [ ] :
     So from that Spring, whence comfort seem'd to come,
     Discomfort swells : Marke King of Scotland, marke,
     No sooner Justice had, with Valour arm'd,
     Compell'd these skipping Kernes to trust their heeles,

But the Norweyan Lord, surveying vantage,
With furbusht Armes, and new supplyes of men,
Began a fresh assault .

3   {*} {This d}ismay'd our Captaines, Macbeth and
[Banquoh ?] {,} {*} as Sparrowes, Eagles ;
Or the Hare, the Lyon :
If I say sooth, I must report they were
As Cannons over-charg'd with double Cracks,
So they doubly redoubled stroakes upon the Foe :
Except they meant to bathe in reeking Wounds,
Or memorize another Golgotha,
I cannot tell : but I am faint,
My Gashes cry for helpe .

At times F's orthography makes the Captaine's pain very evident, as with a) at least eight extra breath-thoughts (marked, and seen first in the second line of the speech and clustering at the opening of F #2), the tiny extra pauses suggesting that he needs to counteract the pain before continuing; and b) at the opening and closing of F #3, where the shaded text shows where F has set the Captaine five short lines, the pauses all pointing to moments of pain that threaten to swamp him as he struggles to finish his story. Most modern editions reduce the five irregular lines to three of almost pure pentameter, thus reducing the last moments of his bravery.

There is also much to suggest that the information is coming out in streams of consciousness rather than as a preplanned report, viz. a) the onrush (modern texts splitting F #1 and #3 into three and F #2 in two); b) the lack of unembellished lines; c) the very few surround phrases; and d) the enormous number of releases throughout (50/34).

• The three surround phrases seem to signify an extra urgency where he needs even more energy to get past the pain, when he describes first the overall situation (" : but all's too weake : ") then the bravery of Macbeth and Banquo who regarded the new wave of enemy forces without fear (" : Or the Hare, the Lyon ;"), and finally his own injuries (": but I am faint, / My Gashes cry for helpe").

• The speech is essentially passionate throughout.

• There is no single moment when emotion dominates the proceedings.

• The only time intellect is paramount comes at the end of F #1, where the Captaine describes how Macbeth beheaded the rebel Macdonwald and "fix'd his Head upon our Battlements" (4/0, the last two and half lines of F #1).

Lady Macbeth's Speeches, I.v: Modern Text

Enter LADY MACBETH, reading a letter.

LADY MACBETH "They met me in the day of success; and I have
learned by the perfect'st° report, they have more in them
than mortal knowledge. When I burned in desire to question
them further, they made themselves air, into which they vanished.
Whiles I stood rapt in the wonder of it, came missives   5
from the King, who all-hailed me Thane of Cawdor; by which
title, before, these Weird Sisters saluted me, and referred me
to the coming on of time, with "Hail, King that shalt be!" This
have I thought good to deliver° thee (my dearest partner of
greatness) that thou might'st not lose the dues of rejoicing by   10
being ignorant of what greatness is promised thee. Lay it to
thy heart, and farewell."
Glamis thou art, and Cawdor, and shalt be
What thou art promised. Yet do I fear° thy nature;
It is too full o' th' milk of human kindness   15
To catch the nearest way. Thou wouldst be great;
Art not without ambition, but without
The illness° should attend it. What thou wouldst highly,°
That wouldst thou holily; wouldst not play false,
And yet wouldst wrongly win. Thou'dst have, great Glamis,   20
That which cries, "Thus thou must do," if thou have it;
And that which rather thou dost fear to do,
Than wishest should be undone. Hie° thee hither,
That I may pour my spirits in thine ear,
And chastise with the valor of my tongue   25
All that impedes thee from the golden round,°
Which Fate and metaphysical° aid doth seem
To have thee crowned withal.°
Enter MESSENGER.
What is your tidings?
MESSENGER The King comes here tonight.
LADY MACBETH   Thou'rt mad to say it.
Is not thy master with him?—who, wer't so,   30
Would have informed° for preparation.

1–12   An actress today will seek a motivation for entering the stage and reading this letter aloud. In Shakespeare's day the young male actor playing the role might not worry about such questions; for him, soliloquy was a convenient and widely accepted stage convention. Yet in all of Shakespeare's works, no other actor has the same burden: this character enters for the very first time, and unannounced, in the middle of reading the letter. The sudden demand for instant reality calls, at least, for absolute confidence. (Compare the easier circumstances of Hotspur in *I Henry IV,* II.iii, and of the lovers in *Love's Labors Lost,* IV.iii and *As You Like It,* III.ii.)

most reliable

Perhaps Lady Macbeth reads aloud because she can scarcely believe the news. Does she imitate her husband's speech, trying to enter into his mind? Are some words stressed as they strike her mind, rather than as they represent her husband's? Does she respond to the gentleness of "my dearest partner in greatness"? Has she read the letter before—several times, perhaps—and now reads it only to mock her husband's extreme caution? The audience knows almost all the facts it relates so its interest will be quickened only by *how* she reads the letter, and especially by what this reveals about herself.

tell

mistrust

wickedness   you especially desire to have

13–28   Syntax, antitheses, and imagery all suggest thoughts that quicken repeatedly into further life as they are given expression. In the play only her husband has an imagination so sensitive, varied, and vivid; yet her speech, unlike many of his, is totally controlled, often very direct and concise. From "Hie thee hither," she moves swiftly and strongly to thoughts of the "golden round" and prophecy fulfilled. She speaks mostly of her husband, guessing at the fears and the response to "holiness" which the audience knows already are part of his reactions to the witches. The two first-person pronouns (ll. 14 and 24) are crucial to the meaning and shape of the soliloquy; the second providing its forward impetus.

hasten

i.e., the crown
supernatural
moreover

Some Lady Macbeths do not doubt success: the determination of Sarah Siddons's "seemed as uncontrollable as fate itself."

sent word

28–38   If Lady Macbeth has responded particularly to what Macbeth has called "more . . . than mortal

MESSENGER So please you, it is true; our thane is coming.
One of my fellows had the speed° of him,
Who, almost dead for breath, had scarcely more
Than would make up his message.
LADY MACBETH   Give him tending,   35
He brings great news.
Exit MESSENGER.
The raven° himself is hoarse
That croaks the fatal entrance of Duncan
Under my battlements. Come, you spirits
That tend° on mortal° thoughts, unsex me here,   40
And fill me, from the crown to the toe, top-full
Of direst cruelty! Make thick my blood,
Stop up th' access and passage to remorse,°
That no compunctious° visitings of nature
Shake my fell° purpose, nor keep peace between
Th' effect and it!° Come to my woman's breasts,   45
And take my milk for gall, you murd'ring ministers,°
Wherever in your sightless° substances
You wait on nature's mischief!° Come, thick night,
And pall thee° in the dunnest° smoke of Hell,
That my keen knife see not the wound it makes,   50
Nor Heaven peep through the blanket of the dark
To cry, "Hold, hold!"
Enter MACBETH.
Great Glamis! Worthy Cawdor!
Greater than both, by the all-hail hereafter!
Thy letters have transported me beyond
This ignorant present, and I feel now   55
The future in the instant.
MACBETH   My dearest love, Duncan comes here tonight.
LADY MACBETH And when goes hence?
MACBETH Tomorrow, as he purposes.
LADY MACBETH   O never
Shall sun that morrow see!
Your face, my thane, is as a book, where men   60
May read strange matters: to beguile the time,
Look like the time,° bear welcome in your eye,
Your hand, your tongue; look like the innocent flower,
But be the serpent under't. He that's coming

outdistanced

bird of ill-omen

attend   murderous

pity
remorseful
cruel
i.e., intervene between
  my purpose and its
  fulfilment
agents
invisible
i.e., the evil-doing inherent in human nature
i.e., cover Duncan
  darkest

i.e., to deceive everyone,
  behave as others do

knowledge" (is this why she started to reread the letter at this point?) and has believed fully in "Fate and metaphysical aid" (l. 27)—and possibly seen her own "spirits" (l. 24) as possessing similar power—she will feel an almost physical shock on the Messenger's first words. "The King" can then mean only Macbeth to her: the other king was not expected, and the second prophecy was waiting for fulfillment. To a less convinced Lady, the news is amazing enough: the letter had not announced Duncan's visit, and now he is coming; and he can be murdered. The abrupt way in which she replies must almost betray the thoughts about murder which have been active under all her words so far in the scene. She despatches the Messenger as soon as she can and then her words have less immediate tension: in her imagination the raven has foretold death for a long time; the castle in which Macbeth has left her has become "my battlements."

38–52 Until "my keen knife" (l. 50), Lady Macbeth need not be fully conscious of her intention to murder. How willingly does she reach this point? Some Lady Macbeths pray to the "spirits" (l. 38) as if already accustomed to be in their presence. But others start more tentatively and use this invocation to summon their own courage, taking upon themselves the entirely new role of murderess. Sex, natural pity and concern, nurturing instincts, an ability to imagine the feelings of others—all have to be offered up before taking hold of the murderous "knife." The soliloquy is as full of tender feelings as it is of cruelty and very palpable horror.

At the close Lady Macbeth takes responsibility boldly—it is "my knife" now, not her husband's—but she is still aware of "Heaven" and of her own transgression. Each actress must choose which thoughts are strongest and whether the soliloquy leaves Lady Macbeth strong in power and self-determination, or nearly exhausted, pulled both ways between ambition and pity.

52–59 Macbeth's entry is timed at the climax of his wife's invocation of spirits and the night. How does he enter? His first words are to be "My dearest love," but he then announces the opportunity to kill

Must be provided for; and you shall put   65
This night's great business into my dispatch,°
Which shall to all our nights and days to come
Give solely° sovereign sway and masterdom.
MACBETH   We will speak further.
LADY MACBETH   Only look up clear;°
To alter favor° ever is to fear.   70
Leave all the rest to me.
Exeunt.

management

to us alone

cheerfully
facial expression

Duncan. Besides, he rode long and fast. For the moment, Lady Macbeth is far less ambiguous: the sight of her husband finds her "transported" to the time when he is king. But she might be putting on a show, the better to pour "her spirits" into his ear (l. 24).

An incomplete verse-line (l. 59) marks a pause as both think of the murder to be committed, and of each other: Macbeth has almost spoken of it in the preceding line; Lady Macbeth does in the following, but depersonalizing the act. How slowly, how unwillingly, have they reached this moment? Or have they rushed toward it, not naming the deed because they are so much in accord—perhaps almost jesting about it?

60–71 Taking the cue from lines 60–61, some Macbeths look shattered by what they foresee; others appear strong and frightening because they have become totally involved, their determination augmented by their wife's complete understanding. At lines 69–70, she assumes that he fears to do what they must do, but that is only what she expected to see in his face. In rehearsal the two actors will find how best to play this scene together; perhaps all that can be said beforehand is that it is intensely intimate, both reading each other's thoughts and feelings.

Two ambiguities must be faced. First, the "night's great business" can be either the feast due to be given to Duncan, or the murder itself. (Lady Macbeth is alone to greet the king in the next scene, but she has already spoken of providing for this responsibility.) Then it is not clear when the two embrace or kiss, or whether they stand apart throughout the scene. The end of line 53 is probably the earliest cue for an intimate greeting; here Laurence Olivier's Macbeth embraced his Lady center stage. "My dearest love" (l. 56) is sometimes followed by a kiss, the rest of that short speech following a close embrace. Sometimes they kiss in the pause after line 59. If it occurs later, after line 70 for example, it will be Lady Macbeth who takes the lead in this and seems to be almost totally in charge of her husband.

Macbeth can start to leave the stage with "We will speak further" or else wait to follow his wife after line 70 or 71. Sometimes they leave together, in close physical contact.

Lady Macbeth's Speeches, I.v: First Folio Texts

1. LADY THEY MET ME IN THE DAY OF SUCCESSE : AND I HAVE

2. LADY GLAMYS THOU ART, AND CAWDOR, AND SHALT BE

3. LADY THE RAVEN HIMSELFE IS HOARSE,

Background: These are Lady Macbeth's (referred to in the first folio simply as "Lady") first series of speeches in the play, all triggered by a letter from her husband telling her of the strange greetings and prophecies, including that of becoming King. Speech #1 deals with the letter itself (the italics being a conventional First Folio method of setting written documents). In speech #2 she unflinchingly faces what weaknesses must be overcome if Macbeth is to become king. In speech #3, following the news that both Macbeth and the current king, Duncan, will arrive at the castle that same day, she appeals to the darker supernatural powers for help.

Style: all solo

Where: somewhere in the castle at Inverness, possibly her private chambers

To Whom: self

1. # of Lines: 12 **Probable Timing:** 0.40 minutes

2. # of Lines: 17 **Probable Timing:** 0.55 minutes

3. # of Lines: 22 **Probable Timing:** 1.10 minutes

THEY MET ME IN THE DAY OF SUCCESSE : AND I HAVE

Lady

1 *They met me in the day of successe: and I have
learn'd by the perfect'st report, they have more in them, [then]
mortall knowledge.*

2   *When I burnt in desire to question them
further, they made themselves Ayre, into which they vanish'd.*

3 *Whiles I stood rapt in the wonder of it, came Missives from
the King, who all hail'd me* Thane *of Cawdor, by which Title*

before, these [weyward] Sisters saluted me, and referr'd me to
the comming on of time, with haile King that shalt be .

4   *This*

have I thought good to deliver thee (my dearest Partner of
Greatnesse) that thou might'st not loose the dues of rejoycing
by being ignorant of what Greatnesse is promis'd thee .

5   *Lay*

it to thy heart, and farewell.

Her immediate response to the various stages of information the letter presents her suggests that she is reading it for the first time or is at last alone where she can read it aloud and react to it for the first time—and though the overall speech seems passionate (10/10 overall), each piece of news seems to bring a different stylistic response.

• Given the circumstances, it's hardly surprising that she starts emotionally (F #1, 0/2), yet—a wonderful sign of her strength of mind throughout—she opens carefully, with two of the first four phrases being unembellished ("and I have learn'd by the perfect'st report, they have more in them,") and the surround phrase that opens the reading of the letter (" . They met me in the day of successe ; ") suggesting great concentration.

• And she remains calm with the information that the Weyward Sisters just disappeared, for with the exception of the "Ayre" they vanished into, this is also unembellished (F #2, 1/1).

• Then her mind becomes very active as she processes how "Missives from the King" confirmed the "Thane of Cawdor" (6/0, F #3's first three lines)—at least until she reads the prophecy that Macbeth will be "King," at which point the first emotion kicks in (1/2, F #3's last line).

• And so comes passion (3/4, F #4) as she reads Macbeth's confirmation that she is now and will in the future be "my dearest Partner of Greatnesse."

• That the last sentence is unembellished is surprising, perhaps suggesting that the news and/or her immediate reaction to it has almost taken her breath away.

GLAMYS THOU ART, AND CAWDOR, AND SHALT BE

Lady

1 [Glamys] thou art, and Cawdor, and shalt be
    What thou art promis'd : yet doe I feare thy Nature,
    It is too full o'th'Milke of [humane] kindnesse,
    To catch the neerest way .

2   Thou would'st be great,
    Art not without Ambition, but without
    The illnesse should attend it .

3   What thou would'st highly,
    That would'st thou holily : would'st not play false,
    And yet would'st wrongly winne .

4 Thould'st have, great [Glamys], that which cryes,
    Thus thou must doe, if thou have it ;
    And that which rather thou do'st feare to doe,
    [Then] wishest should be undone .

5   High thee hither,
    That I may powre my Spirits in thine Eare,
    And chastise with the valour of my Tongue
    All that impeides thee from the Golden Round,
    Which Fate and Metaphysicall ayde doth seeme
    To have thee crown'd withall .

It is only after much analysis of her husband's character, and having found the approach "To have thee crown'd withall," that her passions finally flow.

• The speech starts very carefully, the opening intellectual surround (" . Glamys thou art, and Cawdor, and shalt be / What thou art promis'd : ") not simply summing up all that she knows to date but promising that the Weyward Sisters' prophecy will be fulfilled in full.

• But her concerns that his nature is "too full o'th'Milke of humane kindnesse" are very emotional (2/6, F #1's last two lines), which turns to passion as she so quickly assesses his fundamental flaw: that he wants greatness but is not sufficiently ruthless to achieve it (F #2, 1/1).

- Her further detailing of what she perceives as his weakness now becomes emotional (F #3–4, 1/6), and is immediately thrown into even greater relief with F #3's two surround phrases: " . What thou would'st highly, / would'st thou holily : would'st not play false, / And yet would'st wrongly winne . "

- In F #4 she understands that her manipulative strength will lie in the fact that, though her husband hears "that which cryes, / Thus thou must doe, if thou have it ;" and fears it, he'd rather hear it "Then wishest should be undone." This is underscored by a) the moment of realization linking the two ideas, via the only emotional semicolon in the speech, and b) F #3's recognition of his weakness, marked by F's three irregular shaded lines (6/7 or 8/8 syllables) that suggest a pause before she begins to discover F #4's solution: a pause most modern texts remove by resetting the text as two almost pentameter lines (9 or 10/11), as shown.

- At last, as she realizes how she may manipulate him, passions spring forth (F #5, 7/8) as she envisages stirring him by pouring "my Spirits in thine Eare."

THE RAVEN HIMSELFE IS HOARSE,

Lady

1   The Raven himselfe is hoarse,
    That croakes the fatall entrance of Duncan
    Under my Battlements .

2   Come you Spirits,
    That tend on mortall thoughts, unsex me here,
    And fill me from the Crowne to the Toe, top-full
    Of direst Crueltie : make thick my blood,
    Stop up th'accesse, and passage to Remorse,
    That no compunctious visitings of Nature
    Shake my fell purpose, nor keepe peace betweene
    Th'effect, and [hit] .

3   Come to my Womans Brests,
    And take my Milke for Gall, you [murth'ring] Ministers,
    Where-ever, in your sightlesse substances,
    You wait on Natures Mischiefe .

4   Come thick Night,
  And pall thee in the dunnest smoake of Hell,
  That my keene Knife see not the Wound it makes,
  Nor Heaven peepe through the Blanket of the darke,
  To cry, hold, hold .   *Enter Macbeth.*
5 Great [Glamys], worthy Cawdor,
  Greater [then] both, by the all-haile hereafter,
  Thy Letters have transported me beyond
  This ignorant present, and I feele now
  The future in the instant .

With only one major piece of punctuation and no surround phrases, it would seem that once she starts, rather than controlling the event, her recognition of what happens to her and her need to complete the transformation is what drives the speech—though the onrush after Macbeth's arrival may suggest that she cannot yet control the new being she has become.

• Whether real or symbolic, the opening recognition of the cry of the bird of foreboding (itself a fascinating contrast to the innocent and abundant "temple-haunting martlet" that greeted Duncan and the royal party when they arrived) is voiced passionately (F #1, 3/3), while the first invitation to the "Spirits / That tend on mortall thoughts" to "unsex me" (4/2, F #2's first three lines) becomes more controlled.

• But then the first of two onrushed moments in the speech mark what most modern texts regard as a slight loss of grammatical control (setting a more rational mt. #3), while the ensuing text turns passionate (2/3, the last four lines of F #2)—the two factors suggesting that perhaps the "make thick my blood," and why, is a reaction to what is happening to her rather than an order to continue.

• She seems to reestablish control of self and situation with F #3's "Come to my Womans Brests" (7/3), and, to a lesser extent, in the double request for "thick Night" to come, so she will not see "the Wound" her knife makes, and "Heaven" will not witness the attack on Duncan (F #4, 6/4).

• It may be more of a struggle for her to maintain such control than the modern texts suggest, for F has added four extra breath-thoughts, two in F #2 and one each in F #3–4, suggesting that what follows is of great difficulty for her to endure (", top-full / Of direst Crueltie"; ", and passage to Remorse,") or is very specific to her needs (", in your sightlesse substances"; ", To cry, hold, hold").

- Though most modern texts separate the greeting (mt. #6) and her description of the effect that his letter has had on her (mt. #7), F jams both together, this onrush suggesting a slight loss of control once more as Macbeth appears—again, as with the end of mt. #2, the content of the onrush is passionate (3/2).

Macbeth and Lady Macbeth's Speeches, I.vii: Modern Text

Oboes. Torches. Enter a Sewer,° and divers servants with dishes and service [who pass] over the stage. Then enter MACBETH.

MACBETH If it were done when 'tis done, then 'twere well
It were done quickly. If th' assassination
Could trammel up° the consequence, and catch
With his surcease,° success; that but this blow
Might be the be-all and the end-all-here,   5
But here, upon this bank and shoal of time,
We'd jump° the life to come. But in these cases
We still have judgment° here, that° we but teach
Bloody instructions, which being taught return
To plague th' inventor. This even-handed° justice   10
Commends th' ingredients of our poisoned chalice
To our own lips. He's here in double trust:
First, as I am his kinsman and his subject,
Strong both against the deed; then, as his host,
Who should against his murderer shut the door,
Not bear the knife myself. Besides, this Duncan
Hath borne his faculties° so meek, hath been
So clear° in his great office, that his virtues
Will plead like angels, trumpet-tongued, against
The deep damnation of his taking-off;°
And pity, like a naked, new-born babe
Striding° the blast, or Heaven's cherubins, horsed
Upon the sightless couriers° of the air,
Shall blow the horrid deed in every eye,
That tears shall drown the wind. I have no spur
To prick the sides of my intent, but only
Vaulting ambition, which o'er-leaps itself,
And falls on th'other.°
Enter LADY [MACBETH].
                                     How now? What news?
LADY MACBETH He has almost supped. Why have you left the
chamber?
MACBETH Hath he asked for me?

supervisor

trap in a net, to make
   ineffective
Duncan's death

risk
i.e, we are always
   punished   in that
impartial

wielded his power
blamelessly

murder

bestriding
invisible runners, i.e., the
   winds

i.e., as a rider who vaults
   too far, misses the
   saddle, and falls on the
   other side of the horse

1–28   Music, the carrying of torches, and the service of a great banquet mark the passage of time during which Duncan has been made welcome. Since eight descendants of Banquo are paraded at IV.i.110, a comparable number of actors should be available to put on this show: it can be developed so that it becomes a ritual of peace and plenty. (It might be arranged so that it echoes and offsets the witches' ritual of I.iii.)

Soon the sound of feasting from off-stage—music and laughter, perhaps—is all that is left of this show; and then, when least expected, Macbeth enters, alone for the first time. Much depends on how he enters and speaks. The monosyllables of his first line invite a slow and deliberate delivery; but he speaks about haste, and the way in which the sense of each of the first four lines is not completed until the following line gives an impression of thoughts breaking through ordinary restraints and a sustained forward impetus. Perhaps Macbeth enters hurriedly, as if fleeing from some horror, and then recovers by forcing himself to speak slowly before giving way to the turbulent, hidden pressures which had forced him to leave the table. But often Macbeth will speak slowly throughout this soliloquy, his fear and self-dramatization seeming instinctive and natural to him, a burden that he carries painfully but, in a sense, willingly. Macbeth does not at first mention Duncan by name, and does not speak of his wife; but, after only brief avoidance, the "assassination," "this blow," and "Bloody instructions" identify the center of his torment. Finally he imagines the deed to be a "poisoned chalice" which he must drink as well as his victim (ll. 10–12). It is now that Macbeth becomes more rational and enumerates reasons why Duncan should not be killed; soon he is able to name his victim and to respond to images of peace and pity, even though damnation and cruelty are still strong in his mind and augmented by images of violent tempest.

Commentary on such a soliloquy cannot be precise. The actor has to yield mind and being to its sequence of images, its syntax, and its rhythms and metre, and so strive, with Macbeth, to survive with the sense of what he says always intact. Whether spoken with nerve-wracked speed, or with deep and painful deliberation, the dominant impression will be one of struggle followed by some degree of resolution. "I have

LADY MACBETH   Know you not he has?
MACBETH We will proceed no further in this business.
He hath honoured me of late, and I have bought
Golden opinions from all sorts of people,
Which would° be worn now in their newest gloss,
Not cast aside so soon.
LADY MACBETH   Was the hope drunk
Wherein you dressed yourself? Hath it slept since?
And wakes it now to look so green° and pale
At what it did so freely? From this time,
Such° I account thy love. Art thou afeard
To be the same in thine own act and valor
As thou art in desire? Wouldst thou have that°
Which thou esteem'st the ornament of life,
And live a coward in thine own esteem,
Letting "I dare not" wait upon "I would,"
Like the poor cat i' th' adage?°
MACBETH   Prithee, peace.   45
I dare do all that may become a man;
Who dares do more is none.
LADY MACBETH   What beast was't then
That made you break° this enterprise to me?
When you durst do it, then you were a man;
And, to be more than what you were, you would   50
Be so much more the man. Nor time, nor place
Did then adhere,° and yet you would make both;
They have made themselves, and that their fitness now
Does unmake° you. I have given suck, and know
How tender 'tis to love the babe that milks me;   55
I would, while it was smiling in my face,
Have plucked my nipple from his boneless gums
And dashed the brains out, had I so sworn
As you have done to this.
MACBETH   If we should fail?
LADY MACBETH We fail?   60
But screw your courage to the sticking-place,°
And we'll not fail. When Duncan is asleep
(Whereto the rather shall his day's hard journey
Soundly invite him), his two chamberlains°

should

sickly

i.e., contemptible

i.e., the crown

proverb ("The cat would
    eat fish, but she will not
    wet her feet.")

make known

prove suitable

unnerve

i.e., set your heart firmly
    only on the deed

attendants on the bed-
    chamber

no spur . . ." (l. 25) alters syntax, rhythm, tempo, and pressure of thought and feeling; Macbeth is now sufficiently reflective and calm to respond immediately to his wife's entry.

29–35 The first exchanges are direct and abrupt, as if a great deal is held back, unspoken, on both sides. When Macbeth speaks at greater length, he has made the decision toward which his soliloquy had been leading him. He does this in a single line (l. 31), speaking for both of them. The reasons he proceeds to give for abandoning the murder they had planned are prudential and self-regarding, and it is not clear how completely he identifies himself with these words. Is he protecting his wife from the horror he has suffered? Or has he rediscovered the role of faithful and loyal thane, which had served him well until this time? Or is he afraid to speak once more of the horrors he seeks to escape?

35–62 It is important for actors not to forget who has the longer speeches in this exchange. Lady Macbeth may give time for her husband to reply—twice in line 36, perhaps, and again at lines 38, 39, and 41. Does she pause for him to reply at line 45, or does he break into her speech? Perhaps she pauses only once, after ". . . Such I account thy love" (l. 39); her next question suggests that they have come closer together, for she knows almost exactly how he has "accounted" his own feelings.

Their conflict is settled only after Macbeth protests that he has done all that "a man" should do and this has given her the cue to restore to him the initiative with an opportunity to be "so much more the man" (l. 51). Doing what she sees as an enhancement of his masculinity is what spurs Macbeth to murder, not her taunts of cowardice and weakness.

Interrogation ceases and Lady Macbeth uses a very precise image of her own smiling "babe" to show that nothing would make her stop in what she had sworn to do. After this, Macbeth's "If we should fail" shows that he has again contemplated murder and is ready for concerted action with his wife.

Sarah Siddons, who played the role many times, believed that "such a tender allusion in the midst of her dreadful language" proved that Lady Macbeth "has really felt the maternal yearnings of a mother toward her

Will I with wine and wassail° so convince,°   65
That memory, the warder° of the brain,
Shall be a fume, and the receipt° of reason
A limbeck° only; when in swinish sleep
Their drenched natures lie, as in a death,
What cannot you and I perform upon   70
Th' unguarded Duncan? What not put upon
His spongy officers, who shall bear the guilt
Of our great quell?°
MACBETH   Bring forth men-children only!
For thy undaunted mettle° should compose
Nothing but males. Will it not be received,°   75
When we have marked with blood those sleepy two
Of his own chamber, and used their very daggers,
That they have done't?
LADY MACBETH   Who dares receive it other,°
As we shall make our griefs and clamor roar
Upon his death?
MACBETH   I am settled, and bend up°   80
Each corporal agent° to this terrible feat.
Away, and mock° the time with fairest show;
False face must hide what the false heart doth know.
Exeunt.

strong drink   overcome
watchman
container (i.e., the brain)
still (full of alcoholic
    fumes)

murder

temperament
accepted as true

otherwise

strain
bodily faculty
deceive

babe" and that she used "her very virtues" as the means to taunt her husband into action ("Remarks," 1824). The effect in her performance was of terrifying cruelty and evil. Ellen Terry, however, using a very similar approach, turned Lady Macbeth's words into a "frenzied appeal;" she was so desperate at the sudden paralysis of her husband that she had to "brush away a tear." For Judi Dench's Lady of 1976, the description of her babe was a "steady, screwed-up self-desecration."

Lady Macbeth's "We fail?", with or without the question mark, is a famous crux. For Mrs. Siddons it was "quick and contemptuous," for Ellen Terry a "cry of defiance."

62–82   At this point Henry Irving's Macbeth was seated, and Terry's Lady Macbeth went to kneel at his side and take his hands; and so she explained carefully what should be done, making a common task of "our great quell" (l. 73). But Lady Macbeth, knowing that she has won, may point her advice with ironic humor and keep at a distance from her husband.

Macbeth's exclamation at line 73 is, perhaps, an answer to her lines 54–59. Glen Byan Shaw, who directed Olivier at Stratford-upon-Avon in 1955, believed that the couple had indeed had an only son who had died, and that Macbeth refers here to the grief which still lived within both of them. Alternatively, Macbeth may, in his fashion, be paying a compliment to her for lack of fear. Either way he continues to plan with the same ironic and practical awareness that his wife has just exhibited. One word of agreement from her, and he is "settled:" "we" is replaced with "I" (l. 80), and suggestion with command (ll. 82–83). In giving back the advice he had received at the end of I.iv he is again combining "fair" and "foul" and he does so, with confident rhythm and a conclusive couplet. Almost certainly they leave together; however, Olivier's Macbeth took his Lady's hand "without looking at her."

Toward the end of this scene, sounds of the off-stage banquet are sometimes heard again; these can lend irony to Lady Macbeth's lines 79–80 and give a cue for Macbeth's reference to "fairest show" (l. 82); the "terrible fear" (l. 81) is given sharper meaning if Duncan's presence is made manifestly real by sounds of light-hearted revels at that very moment.

Macbeth and Lady Macbeth's Speeches, I.vii:
First Folio Texts

**MACBETH   IF IT WERE DONE, WHEN 'TIS DONE,
THEN 'TWER WELL,**

Background: With his wife pushing him to assassinate Duncan, Macbeth explores all the possible reasons pro and con, realising there are none "pro" except his own ambition.

Style: solo

Where: Inverness castle, somewhere close to the ongoing banquet

To Whom: self, and audience

# of Lines: 28 **Probable Timing:** 1.30 minutes

Macbeth

1   If it were done, when 'tis done, then 'twer well,
     It were done quickly : If th'Assassination
     Could trammell up the Consequence, and catch
     With his surcease, Successe : that but this blow
     Might be the be all, and the end all .

2   Heere,
     But heere, upon this Banke and [Schoole] of time,
     Wee'ld jumpe the life to come .

3   But in these Cases,
     We still have judgement heere, that we but teach
     Bloody Instructions, which being taught, returne
     To plague th'Inventer, This even-handed Justice
     Commends th'Ingredience of our poyson'd Challice
     To our owne lips .

4   Hee's heere in double trust ;
First, as I am his Kinsman, and his Subject,
Strong both against the Deed : Then, as his Host,
Who should against his [Murtherer] shut the doore,
Not beare the knife my selfe .

5   Besides, this Duncane
Hath borne his Faculties so meeke ; hath bin
So cleere in his great Office, that his Vertues
Will pleade like Angels, Trumpet-tongu'd against
The deepe damnation of his taking off :
And Pitty, like a naked New-borne-Babe,
Striding the blast, or Heavens Cherubin, hors'd
Upon the sightlesse Curriors of the Ayre,
Shall blow the horrid deed in every eye,
That teares shall drowne the winde .

6   I have no Spurre
To pricke the sides of my intent, but onely
Vaulting Ambition, which ore-leapes it selfe,
And falles on th'other .

This is often played as quiet rational exploration, but F's orthography shows just how much of an intellectual/emotional roller-coaster Macbeth undergoes in trying to find a valid reason to justify his murderous intent.

• The quiet of the only two virtually monosyllabic and unembellished passages in the text underscore Macbeth's desire, and the quietness is made all the more noteworthy by forming the bulk of the first sentence in the speech:

> . If it were done, when 'tis done, then 'twer well, /
> It were done quickly : . . . /
> : that but this blow /
> Might be the be all, and the end all .

• However, the calm is only momentary, for the description of Duncan's death as an "Assassination" (by all accounts a Shakespeare-invented word) intellectually breaks the calm (4/2, the two lines between F #1's two colons).

• And while F #2's response to the idea that if the deed were all Macbeth would jump at it is surprisingly strongly emotional (2/6), the F #3 realization that, by example, his killing of Duncan could easily lead to his own death becomes very passionate (7/6 in just five lines).

• Fascinatingly, expressing two of society's reasons why he should not kill Duncan seems to greatly disturb Macbeth, for both are expressed as emotional surround phrases

> . Hee's heere in double trust ; /
> First, as I am his Kinsman, and his Subject, /
> Strong both against the Deed :

> . Besides, this Duncane /
> Hath borne his Faculties so meeke ;

• The struggle between Macbeth's intellect and emotion/passion continues, for, not surprisingly, while the idea of breaking that trust ("Hee's heere in double trust") and the act of killing him ("Not beare the knife my selfe.") trigger his emotions (0/2 twice, in the opening and closing of F #4), what is sandwiched between is an intellectual assessment (6/1 in just three lines) that he has a chivalric double duty to protect Duncan.

• As he voices Duncan's excellent qualities, which again should protect him, Macbeth is moved to passion (6/6, F #5's first four and half lines).

• The realization that Duncan's death will generate such an outcry of "Pitty" becomes slightly more intellectual (F #5's next three lines 7/5), with the fact that all will know of Macbeth's deed striking him with icy certainty via the unembellished "Shall blow the horrid deed in every eye"—the resultant "teares" being known world-wide, since the deed "shall drowne the winde," becoming emotional (0/3).

• As he realizes that there is no reason to kill Duncan except for his own "Vaulting Ambition" to become king, the emotion flows free (F #6, 2/6).

1. Lady   Was the hope drunke, / Wherein you drest your selfe ?

2. Lady   What Beast was't {*} / That made you breake this enterprize to me ?

Background: Having realized there is no legitimate or honest reason for killing Duncan, Macbeth informs his wife "we will proceed no further in this Businesse." These two speeches comprise the bulk of her eventually successful rhetoric, which keeps him to the proposed task in hand, for he eventually responds not just with the admiring "Bring forth Men-Children onely," but "I am settled, and bend up / Each corporall Agent to this terrible Feat."

Style: as part of a two-handed scene

Where: Inverness castle, somewhere close to the ongoing banquet

To Whom: Macbeth

1. # of Lines: 11   **Probable Timing:** 0.40 minutes

2. # of Lines: 26   **Probable Timing:** 1.15 minutes

Was the hope drunke, / Wherein you drest your selfe ?

Lady

1   Was the hope drunke,
     Wherein you drest your selfe ?

2   Hath it slept since ?

3   And wakes it now to looke so greene, and pale,
     At what it did so freely ?

4   From this time,
     Such I account thy love .

5   Art thou affear'd
To be the same in thine owne Act, and Valour,
As thou art in desire ?
6   Would'st thou have that
Which thou esteem'st the Ornament of Life,
And live a Coward in thine owne Esteeme ?
Letting I dare not, wait upon I would,
Like the poore Cat i'th'Addage .

This comes from one of the trickiest sequences facing any actress in the whole of Shakespeare—for the temptation is to play it as an emotional attack from the outset, whereas F's opening establishes a struggle to maintain control, as if she were trying to avoid unnecessarily antagonizing him, unless she has to.

• The opening sentence is emotional, the two released words ("drunke" and "selfe") coming at the end of each phrase, suggesting a careful posing of a necessary question and a great care to maintain control (0/2, F #1).

• Signs of her control succeeding can be seen in the unembellished, monosyllabic, and very short F #2 ("Hath it slept since?"), though while F #3 is as equally emotionally careful as F #1 (0/2), the two released words coming in the first phrase ("looke so greene") might indicate that self-control is becoming a little more difficult to maintain.

• Yet the calm of unembellishment is regained with the end of F #3 and the short F #4 (" : At what it did so freely? From this time, / Such I account thy love."), though the extra breath-thoughts that now begin to occur suggest that this reestablished control does not come without another struggle.

• And then the releases start to flow: 8/7 overall in the last six and a half lines, however, the patterns shift quite interestingly, according to the question/tactic being used to gain any response from her husband. F #5's fear-based questioning is emotional (2/3); her challenging just how deep his desire is for the "Ornament of Life" switches to intellect (2/0, F #6's first one and half lines); and then, whether deliberately as a rhetorical tactic or unconsciously, the final cowardice blow is a passionate 4/4 (F #6's last three lines).

WHAT BEAST WAS'T {*} / THAT MADE YOU BREAKE THIS ENTERPRIZE TO ME ?

Lady

1 What Beast was't {*}
   That made you breake this enterprize to me ?

2 When you durst do it, then you were a man :
   And to be more [then] what you were, you would
   Be so much more the man .

3   Nor time, nor place
   Did then adhere, and yet you would make both :
   They have made themselves, and that their fitnesse now
   Do's unmake you .

4   I have given Sucke, and know
   How tender 'tis to love the Babe that milkes me,
   I would, while it was smyling in my Face,
   Have pluckt my Nipple from his Bonelesse Gummes,
   And dasht the Braines out, had I so sworne
   As you have done to this .

   _____

5 {*}   {S}crew your courage to the sticking place,
   And wee'le not fayle : when Duncan is asleepe,
   (Whereto the rather shall his dayes hard Journey
   Soundly invite him) his two Chamberlaines
   Will I with Wine, and Wassell, so convince,
   That Memorie, the Warder of the Braine,
   Shall be a Fume, and the Receit of Reason
   A Lymbeck onely : when in Swinish sleepe,
   Their drenched Natures lyes as in a Death,
   What cannot you and I performe upon
   Th'unguarded Duncan ?

6   What not put upon
      His spungie Officers ? who shall beare the guilt
      Of our great quell .

The trickiness of the previous speech continues into this one, as Macbeth's wife seeks to influence him without antagonizing him.

• The speech opens very carefully, for after F #1's single striking capital release "Beast" (building on her previous image comparing Macbeth to the "poore Cat i'th'Addage" and thus less than a man, an appallingly demeaning insult to any Elizabethan) comes the cunning emotional release "enterprize," suggesting that their ascending to the throne—by whatever means—is merely a business proposition).

• The care with which she is trying to win him by rational argument (and very strong images) rather than off-putting emotion can be clearly seen in F #2's and nearly all of F #3's next four and a half lines of apparently reasonable debate, which is couched in three very rare unembellished surround phrases (and is, save for the one word "adhere," monosyllabic, too):

> . When you durst do it, then you were a man : /
> And to be more then what you were, you would /
> Be so much more the man . Nor time, nor place /
> Did then adhere, and yet you would make both : / . . .

• This control does not last, for the end of F #3 (the time's "fitnesse") first plunges her into passion as she proves her valor to shame him into action (7/7, F #4), and then, in attempting to forestall his fear of failure (0/2, F #5's opening surround phrase "Screw your courage to the sticking place / And wee'le not fayle") she momentarily becomes emotional.

• That the full planning of the details from the moment "when Duncan is asleepe" and her question "What cannot you and I performe upon / Th'unguarded Duncan?" excites her can be seen in her sudden, enormous onrushed release (16/9, F #5's last nine lines), though whether the passion stems from the idea itself or in trying to get Macbeth to see and grasp the possibilities is up to each actor to explore: this onrush is removed by most modern texts setting two more rational sentences: mt. #6 for why Duncan will sleep, mt. #7 for what they can then do to him.

• Indeed, most modern texts regard F's final sentence as ungrammatical: as set F, seems to suggest that at the very last moment her control slips just a little, yet the immediacy of the circumstances and the urgency of her final F #6 extra sentence demand (". What not put upon / His spungie Officers ? who shall beare the guilt / Of our great quell .") is underscored by a) by being set as two surround phrases, b) the question mark acting as a link (here functioning as the modern exclamation mark), and c) the slight emotion involved (1/2), much more so than by the new modern rationality.

Porter's Speech, II.iii: Modern Text

Enter a Porter. Knocking within.

PORTER Here's a knocking indeed! If a man were porter of Hell
gate, he should have old° turning the key. *(Knock)* Knock,
knock, knock. Who's there, i' th' name of Beelzebub?° Here's
a farmer that hanged himself on th' expectation of plenty:°
come in, farmer; have napkins° enough about you, here   5
you'll sweat for't. *(Knock)* Knock, knock. Who's there, i' th'
other devil's name? Faith, here's an equivocator° that could
swear in both the scales against either scale, who committed
treason enough for God's sake, yet could not equivocate to
heaven: come in, equivocator. *(Knock)* Knock, knock,   10
knock. Who's there? Faith, here's an English tailor come hither
for stealing out of a French hose:° come in, tailor, here you
may roast your goose. *(Knock)* Knock, knock. Never at quiet.
What are you?—but this place is too cold for Hell. I'll devil
porter it no further; I had thought to have let in some of all   15
professions that go the primrose° way to th' everlasting bonfire.
(Knock) Anon, anon; I pray you, remember the porter.
He opens the gate.

plenty of
Prince of Devils
    (Matthew 12:24)
i.e., a farmer who hoarded
    grain but found, with
    a good harvest in view,
    that prices would go
    down and he would be
    ruined
handkerchiefs
one who speaks with
    duplicity
full round breeches (a
    tailor could cheat by
    skimping the amount of
    cloth he used)
flowery, and so alluring

1–17 While the stage is still empty, knocking is heard again and then the Porter stumbles on. There has been no other person like him in the play before, unless among the ranks of silent attendants and soldiers. If played by Armin, the famous clown of the King's Men for whom the Fool in *Lear* was probably written, his very appearance still dazed from sleep and drinking the night before (see ll. 20–21), or his very first words, could have been sufficient to raise a laugh from the audience. But although he has been given his solo "spot," with the role of "Porter of Hell gate" to enact and opportunity for ludicrous imitations of all the people he imagines to be going to Hell, the Porter of Macbeth's castle is much more than a routine funny-man. He recognizes that he is tortured himself ("Never at quiet") and then runs out of invention, opens the gates and asks for a tip (and in another sense asks that his catalogue of vice be remembered—greed, equivocation and lechery).

Actors today either enjoy or hate this scene, and critics are usually strongly for or against how it is played. (Critics mention it far more extensively than its size in the text would seem to warrant.) In its context in the play, the most important thing to achieve may be the impression of a man who takes his own time and goes his own way, and yet is driven by the continual knocking off-stage (which probably grows in sound and impatience). Further, he is seen to have been celebrating the king's visit by heavy drinking the night before, and the time is established early on a very "cold" morning (see l. 14).

Failing to make the scene "work" any other way, some actors play the Porter as a clown who is never successfully funny; or one who is funny only to his own way of thinking; or one who spends the entire first speech searching for the key to the gate, or yawning, or drinking, or preparing to urinate.

In early performances, the topicality of this opening speech, reflecting Jacobean English life, may have been one of its most notable features: the Porter brought the accents and concerns of everyday life to the tragedy set in a remote and, in some ways, barbarous Scotland.

Porter's Speech, II.iii: First Folio Text

PORTER   HERE'S A KNOCKING INDEEDE : IF A MAN WERE

Background: Macduff and Lenox have arrived to escort Duncan on his customary morning ride. It was their knocking that so disturbed the Macbeths. The Porter, in his only scene in the play, seems to be taking his own sweet time to let the visitors in.

Style: solo

Where: the courtyard of Inverness castle

To Whom: self, those beyond the gate, and the audience

Note: For clarity this text bolds and brackets when F shows "Knock" as a stage direction rather than spoken dialogue from the Porter. In the original setting, F distinguished the stage direction via an italicized font.

Porter

1   Here's a knocking indeede : if a man were
     Porter of Hell Gate, hee should have old turning the
     Key . [**Knock**]

2   Knock, Knock, Knock .

3   Who's there
     i'th'name of Belzebub ?

4   Here's a Farmer, that hang'd
     himselfe on th'expectation of Plentie : Come in time, have
     Napkins enow about you, here you'le sweat for't . [**Knock**]

5   Knock, knock .

6   Who's there in th'other Devils Name ?

7   Faith here's an Equivocator, that could sweare in both
     the Scales against eyther Scale, who committed Treason
     enough for Gods sake, yet could not equivocate to Hea-
     ven : oh come in, Equivocator . [**Knock**]

8   Knock,
     Knock, Knock .

9   Who's there ?

10   'Faith here's an English
     Taylor come hither, for stealing out of a French Hose :
     Come in Taylor, here you may rost your Goose . [**Knock**]

11   Knock, [ ] Knock .

12   Never at quiet : What are you ? but this
place is too cold for Hell .

13 Ile Devill-Porter it no further :
I had thought to have let in some of all Professions, that
goe the Primrose way to th'everlasting Bonfire . [Knock]

14 Anon, anon, I pray you remember the Porter .

Quite fascinatingly, despite the entertainment value of the piece and the-woken-very-early-in-the-morning-when-I-supposedly-have-a-hang-over circumstances, the Porter remains in strong intellectual control throughout (34/11 overall) and there isn't a single section where passion or emotion gets the better of him, suggesting that no matter what his status and condition, he is a very centered and knowledgeable man.

• With F #1's surround phrase opening " . Here's a knocking in-deede : ", it seems the knocking has got to the Porter right from the outset, especially since F #1 is regarded as an ungrammatical onrush by most modern texts, which usually split it in two.

• However, he stays in wonderful intellectual control for the first four sentences (11/3 the opening six lines)—the one distinction between the F setting and modern texts is that F #4's onrush is split into three, thus the modern texts create a more rational, hard-working character than his F counterpart.

• Then comes F #5's very short, unembellished, monosyllabic sentence "Knock, knock."—the quiet perhaps suggesting that the knocking is getting to him again, a pattern to be repeated twice more with F #8–9 and #11.

• And following F #6's intellectual challenge (2/0) the first tiny tinge of emotion creeps in as the Porter faces what many Elizabethans had just been taught to hate via a public and inflammatory political trial—an "Equivocator" (F #7, 7/3)—and there's a tiny bit more as he faces down the imaginary thieving "English Taylor" (F #10, 6/2).

• Then, with F #12 and the opening of F #13 being voiced as four consecutive surround phrases—

. Never at quiet : What are you ? but this
place is too cold for Hell . Ile Devill-Porter it no further :

—it appears that something in his imagination seems to disturb the Porter (or perhaps his unspecified reaction—mock-horror, perhaps?—is a game being played with an unsuspecting audience member).

• But then he recovers control (4/1, the last three lines of the speech) for the summation before admitting those who have disturbed him.

Macbeth's Speech, III.i: Modern Text

MACBETH   Go, bid thy mistress, when my drink is ready,
She strike upon the bell. Get thee to bed.   *Exit [servant]*.
Is this a dagger which I see before me,
The handle toward my hand? Come, let me clutch thee:—
I have thee not, and yet I see thee still.   35
Art thou not, fatal° vision, sensible°
To feeling as to sight? Or art thou but
A dagger of the mind, a false creation
Proceeding from the heat-oppressèd brain?
I see thee yet, in form as palpable   40
As this which now I draw.
Thou marshall'st me the way that I was going,
And such an instrument I was to use.—
Mine eyes are made the fools o' th' other senses,
Or else worth all the rest.° —I see thee still;   45
And on thy blade and dudgeon,° gouts° of blood,
Which was not so before. There's no such thing;
It is the bloody business which informs°
Thus to mine eyes. —Now o'er the one half-world
Nature seems dead, and wicked dreams abuse°   50
The curtained sleep. Witchcraft celebrates
Pale Hecate's offerings;° and withered murder,
Alarumed° by his sentinel, the wolf,
Whose howl's his watch,° thus with his stealthy pace,
With Tarquin's ravishing strides,° towards his design   55
Moves like a ghost. Thou sure and firm-set Earth,
Hear not my steps, which way they walk, for fear
The very stones prate of my whereabout,
And take the present horror from the time,
Which now suits with it.° Whiles I threat, he lives: 60
Words to the heat of deeds too cold breath gives.
I go, and it is done; the bell invites me.
Hear it not, Duncan, for it is a knell
That summons thee to Heaven or to Hell.   *Exit*.

31–64 Having arranged for a signal to be given, Macbeth gives order for it now, and then turns toward the door of Duncan's bedchamber. He is appalled by what he sees; and, since the audience sees nothing, this is a particular difficulty for the actor, coming without preparation. First he questions, but then in a line which overflows the measure of the normal pentameter he has accepted the illusion. Line 34 can be either forced within usual bounds, a burst of impetuous energy, or spoken as two half-lines of verse, with a silence between them, and another after he has failed to clutch the dagger.

Macbeth must talk to the illusion. He must draw a real dagger, and find that this is no more real than one which marshalls him to Duncan's bedchamber. At line 46, he must see "gouts of blood" on the blade, "which was not so before." He is completely convinced by the "air-drawn dagger" (the phrase is Lady Macbeth's at III.iv.61), although he tries to rid himself of the belief repeatedly; he not only tries to talk himself out of this "vision," he also fights it in silence (see the incomplete verse-line, 41). For Ian McKellen, playing Macbeth at Stratford-upon-Avon in 1976, "the sighting of the dagger had a steely, obsessive quality; the essential realism of the man experiencing the vision [being] as evident in the grimly determined snatchings with which he sought to master it by reducing the dagger to actuality, as in the emphasis of his final dismissal of it: 'there's no such thing'" (*Shakespearean Criticism,* vol. 20).

In contrast, Olivier in 1955 spoke "with a sort of broken quiet, only the sudden shrillness of 'Mine eyes are made the fools o' th' other senses' and 'There's no such thing' revealing the intolerable tension that strains the speaker" *(Shakespeare Survey).*

Having dispelled the dagger, Macbeth only becomes aware of a more pervasive evil (ll. 49ff.). In Olivier's performance his voice "sank to a drugged whisper and, speaking, Macbeth moved, as in a dream, towards Duncan's room, but with his face turned away from it." However, some Macbeths are entirely still now, until they hear the bell which Lady Macbeth strikes from off-stage (see ll. 31–32). Albert Finney's Macbeth at the National Theatre, London in 1978, spoke the concluding couplet with the renewed energy its rhythms suggest, as if relieved to be in action at last. Other Macbeths leave desperate and damned, almost mindlessly fulfilling their part in the murder because that is the only way they can do so.

ominous   perceptible to the senses

i.e., are deluding me, fooled by other senses, or else they report truly, and are thus worth all the others
handle
drops
takes visible shape
deceive
offerings made to Hecate, goddess of witchcraft and moonlight
roused to action
signal
(alluding to the Roman tyrant's rape of Lucretia, wife of Collatinus)
(Macbeth relishes his own sense of horror, which fortifies his resolve)

Macbeth's Speech, III.i: First Folio Text

MACBETH   GOE BID THY MISTRESSE, WHEN MY DRINKE IS READY,

Background: Macbeth now steels himself to do the deed. One note: just as a possible metamorphosis took place for Lady Macbeth, here there is perhaps one for him here too—notice that after sentence #8, where he refuses to accept the (conscience-driven?) warning of the blood-stained dagger, he is suddenly able to sense and even hear the "halfe World" of witches and their agents, a sense that grows stronger and leads to ever increasingly reckless and less-than-humanity-driven behavior as the play wears on.

Style: solo

Where: the castle at Inverness, probably the battlements

To Whom: self, the "imaginary" dagger, and the audience

# of Lines: 34   **Probable Timing:** 1.40 minutes

Macbeth

1   Goe bid thy Mistresse, when my drinke is ready,
   She strike upon the Bell .

2   Get thee to bed . *[Exit{Servant}]*

3   Is this a Dagger, which I see before me,
   The Handle toward my Hand ?

4   Come, let me clutch thee :
   I have thee not, and yet I see thee still .

5   Art thou not fatall Vision, sensible
   To feeling, as to sight ? or art thou but
   A Dagger of the Minde, a false Creation,
   Proceeding from the heat-oppress'd Braine ?

6   I see thee yet, in forme as palpable,
   As this which now I draw .

7   Thou marshall'st me the way that I was going,
   And such an Instrument I was to use .

8 Mine Eyes are made the fooles o'th'other Sences,

Or else worth all the rest : I see thee still ;

And on thy Blade, and Dudgeon, Gouts of Blood,

Which was not so before .

9   There's no such thing :

It is the bloody Businesse, which informes

Thus to mine Eyes .

10   Now o're the one halfe World

Nature seemes dead, and wicked Dreames abuse

The Curtain'd sleepe : Witchcraft celebrates

Pale Heccats Offrings : and wither'd [Murther],

Alarum'd by his Centinell, the Wolfe,

Whose howle's his Watch, thus with his stealthy pace,

With Tarquins ravishing [sides], towards his designe

Moves like a Ghost .

11   Thou [sowre] and firme-set Earth

Heare not my steps, which [they may] walke, for feare

Thy very stones prate of my where-about,

And take the present horror from the time,

Which now sutes with it .

12   Whiles I threat, he lives :

Words to the heat of deedes too cold breath gives .

Bell rings.

13 I goe, and it is done : the Bell invites me .

14 Heare it not, Duncan, for it is a Knell,

That summons thee to Heaven, or to Hell .

The speech is remarkable in that Macbeth initially shows enormous self-control when faced with the "fatall Vision" of the dagger, yet once he decides he knows from whence it comes and he gets side-tracked into the "one halfe World" his control disappears until the bell (the signal from his wife) reminds him of the need for immediate action.

• For a simple servant dismissal, Macbeth is surprisingly passionate (2/3, F #1), which he may suddenly realize, for F #2's follow-up "Get thee to bed." is short, monosyllabic, and unembellished.

• And this control is maintained at the sight of the "Dagger" for the first questioning of what he sees is staunchly/steadfastly intellectual (F #3, 3/0), and the attempt to grasp it and his response to his inability to do so is very quiet:

> . Come, let me clutch thee : /
> I have thee not, and yet I see thee still . /
> Art thou not . . . , sensible /
> To feeling, as to sight ?

Whether the unembellished calm is enforced or natural, given the circumstances, his control is remarkable, especially considering the releases of the previous soliloquy.

• Though emotion makes itself felt as he faces the possibility that the dagger stems from his own fevered brain he nevertheless still stays in intellectual control (4/2, F #5's last two lines)—until the dagger still remains visible and motions him towards Duncan's chamber when, for a moment, Macbeth's emotions get the better of him (1/2, F #6–7).

• Even while not knowing what to believe he still maintains his reason (F #8, 6/1), though it takes two surround phrases—one emotional and semicolon-created: " . Mine Eyes are made the fooles o'th'other Sences, / Or else worth all the rest : I see thee still ; "

• However, the passion of his surround-phrase refusal to accept the dagger as real (F #9, 2/2: " . There's no such thing : / It is the bloody Businesse, which informes / Thus to mine Eyes .") completely blows his self-control, for presuming the vision is of his own creating (and thus refusing any possibility of his conscience and/or divine intervention preventing him from destroying himself) leads him into a sudden flurry of passion (12/8 in F #10's eight and a half lines) as he experiences for the very first time the exhilarating half-world linking man and the supernatural, the key understanding highlighted by yet another surround phrase " : Witchcraft celebrates / Pale Heccats Offrings :"

• The determination that no one should hear him approach Duncan is very emotional initially (1/5, F #11's first two lines), while the notion/fear that everything will give him away suddenly causes him to go very quiet: "Thy very stones prate of my where-about, / And take the present horror from the time, / Which now sutes with it."

- Yet his strength enables him to go beyond his fear and he returns to determined surround phrase control as he realizes he must act (F #12, 0/1). The sentence is also unembellished save for the one key word "deedes": " . Whiles I threat, he lives : / Words to the heat of deedes too cold breath gives ."

- The final determination to go on is strongly intellectual once more (5/2, F #13–14); the understanding that all is ready and that if he just goes to Duncan everything will be achieved is also voiced via yet more surround phrases: F #13's " . I goe, and it is done : the Bell invites me ."

Macbeth's Speech, V.v: Modern Text

MACBETH She should have died hereafter;°
There would have been a time for such a word.°
Tomorrow, and tomorrow, and tomorrow,
Creeps in this petty pace from day to day,   20
To the last syllable of recorded time;
And all our yesterdays have lighted fools
The way to dusty death. Out, out, brief candle!
Life's but a walking shadow, a poor player
That struts and frets his hour upon the stage   25
And then is heard no more. It is a tale
Told by an idiot, full of sound and fury,
Signifying nothing.°

at some more appropriate
   time
announcement

(biblical echoes resonate
   in these lines; see for
   example Psalms 22:15
   and 39.7, Job 14.1–2
   and 18.6)

17–28 Incomplete verse-lines mark the silences as Seyton delivers his news and Macbeth begins to respond. Every actor will recognize the huge challenge of the speech which follows this transition: here Macbeth revalues his every word and action, his whole life, and those of every man and woman. Each actor must find how best to act it, whether with increasing energy and decisiveness as he reduces life to a bitter, stupid joke, or with a deep regret which fuels a new sense of loneliness and endless suffering.

The rhythms of the speech insist on calm reflection after the repeated *tomorrow*s, as if some part of his mind finds peace in rejecting the present's pressing concerns. Then "Out, out, brief candle!" is an immediate imperative, whether calling for death or remembering the light which his wife had kept "by her continually" (V.i.18).

"She should have died hereafter . . ." (ll. 17–18) is a particular problem and how this is solved will set the pitch of the whole speech. Either Macbeth finds himself insensible to his wife's death or he is so struck with loss that this is an attempt to cover up the silent suffering which can have no adequate expression in words.

Macbeth's Speech, V.v: First Folio Text

MACBETH   SHE SHOULD HAVE DY'DE HEEREAFTER ;

Background: This is Macbeth's response to the news "The Queene (my Lord) is dead."

Style: solo, in front of one other person

Where: the castle at Dunsinane

To Whom: self, audience, in front of Seyton

# of Lines: 12   **Probable Timing:** 0.40 minutes

Macbeth

1   She should have dy'de heereafter ;

    There would have beene a time for such a word :

    To morrow, and to morrow, and to morrow,

    Creepes in this petty pace from day to day,

    To the last Syllable of Recorded time :

    And all our yesterdayes, have lighted Fooles

    The way to dusty death .

2   Out, out, breefe Candle,

    Life's but a walking Shadow, a poore Player,

    That struts and frets his houre upon the Stage,

    And then is heard no more .

3   It is a Tale

    Told by an Ideot, full of sound and fury

    Signifying nothing .

Following the announcement of his wife's death, his lack of further words about her need not mean that he is not moved, for the speech opens with two emotional surround phrases (created by the only semi-colon of the speech): " . She should have dy'de heereafter ; / There would have beene a time for such a word : ". The emotional semicolon is enhanced by the emotion of the first two lines (0/3).

- The "petty pace" that is to continue "from day to day" is expressed passionately (3/3), though very interestingly the preceding " To morrow, and to morrow, and to morrow" that triggers this sequence is eerily and bleakly unembellished, a conclusion matched by his final unembellished summation of the speech.

- The sequence continues passionately as he suggests, first, that his life should finish ("Out, out, breefe Candle"), and then in realizing that as a consequence, life is but a "walking Shadow" with a very short life span to come (F #2, 4/3).

- F #3's despairing assessment that life is a "Tale / Told by an Ideot" is passionate (2/1), and then comes the final unembellished conclusion—"full of sound and fury / Signifying nothing ."—as if Macbeth's realization of life's bleakness is echoed in his delivery.